FAST START FOR EARLY READERS - KINDERGARTEN

Written and illustrated by Paul Mackie.
Cover Picture graphic: - shutterstock

Library and Archives Canada Cataloguing in Publication

Mackie, Paul - Author
FAST START FOR EARLY READERS - KINDERGARTEN

ISBN 978-1-988986-14-2

Copyright© 2019 by Paul Mackie
All rights reserved. No part of this book may be reproduced, or utilized in any form, or by any means, electronic, mechanical or photocopying (unless stated in this book), without permission in writing from the Author.
Contact author: **educationalchildsplay@gmail.com**

http://howtoteachchildrentoread.ca

The methods presented in this book are intended to help children learn how to read and are not a guarantee of success that a child will learn how to read or write.

All methods in this book are the ideas of the author and do not represent the views of other books, authors and their methods.

Contents

HOW TO TEACH YOUR PRE-SCHOOL CHILD TO READ	4
TEACH YOUR PRE-SCHOOL CHILD TO READ METHOD	5
THE LETTER "m"	6
THE LETTER "a"	8
THE LETTER "n"	10
THE LETTERS "m" "a" "n"	12
THE LETTER "r"	14
THE LETTERS "m" "a" "n" "r"	16
THE LETTER "f"	18
THE LETTER "s"	20
THE LETTER "e"	22
THE LETTERS "m" "a" "n" "r" "f" "s" "e"	24
THE LETTER "t"	26
LETTER REVISION PRACTICE	28
THE LETTER "l"	30
THE LETTER "g"	32
THE LETTER "c"	34
THE LETTER "k"	36
THE LETTER "b"	38
LETTER REVISION PRACTICE	40
THE LETTER "i"	42
THE LETTER "h"	44
THE LETTER "d"	46
LETTER REVISION PRACTICE	48
THE LETTER "p"	50
LETTER REVISION PRACTICE	52
THE LETTER "o"	54
THE LETTER "j"	56
THE LETTER "w"	58
LETTER REVISION PRACTICE	60
THE LETTER "u"	62
THE LETTER "v"	64
THE LETTER "q"	66
THE LETTER "x"	68
THE LETTER "y"	70
THE LETTER "z"	72
LETTER REVISION PRACTICE	74

5 VOWEL SOUNDS	76
VOWEL SOUNDS – "a" – "e" – "i" – "o" – "u"	82
SHORT AND LONG VOWELS	88
NEW SOUND - "s" = "z"	90
NEW SOUND - "ch"	92
NEW SOUND - "sh"	94
NEW SOUND - "th"	96
NEW SOUND - "wh"	98
NEW SOUND - THREE SOUNDS OF "y"	100
NEW SOUND - "ai" and "ay"= long "a"	102
NEW SOUND - "ea" and "ee"= long "e"	104
NEW SOUND - "ie" and "igh"= long "i"	106
NEW SOUND - "oa" and "oe"= long "o"	108
NEW SOUND - "ow" and "ou"= "ow"	110
NEW SOUND-("ar" "ear" "ir" "or" "ur") = "er"	112
NEW SOUND - "kn" = "n"	114
NEW SOUND - "gn" = "n	116
NEW SOUND - "gu" = "g"	118
NEW SOUND - "wr" = "r"	120
NEW SOUND - "mb" = "m"	122
NEW SOUND "ai"= short "i" – "ea"= long "a" "ea"= short "e" – "ie"= long "e"	124
NEW SOUND – "g" = "j" - "dge"	126
NEW SOUND "oo"-"oe"-"ue"-"ou""ew"= "oo"	128
NEW SOUND "oi" - "oy"	130
NEW SOUND "aw"-"au"-"augh"-"ough"= "aw"	132
NEW SOUND "sh"	134
NEW SOUND "ph" and "gh" = "f"	136
NEW SOUND "ei" - "ey" - "ew" - "eu" - "eigh"	138
NEW SOUND-"ed"="ed"-"ed"="d"-"ed"="t"	140
NEW SOUND - "ang"-"ong"-"ung"-"eng"	142
THIS BOOK TEACHES 76 SOUNDS	144
TEACHING TIPS	145
PHONIC RULES and SIGHT WORDS:	150
OTHER BOOKS BY THE AUTHOR	157
ABOUT THE AUTHOR	162

HOW TO TEACH YOUR PRE-SCHOOL CHILD TO READ

THE METHOD
Start teaching your child the lowercase (short) sound of English alphabet letters (phonemes – which are speech sounds); this involves "ear", "tongue", "eye" and "word building" training.

Step 1. Ear Training - Begin by slowly sounding out words of things you want your child to do: "Bring me a c-u-p." – "Show me something r-e-d." - "c-l-a-p your hands." - "Bring me a p-e-n."

Step 2. Tongue Training – Sound out a word slowly "c-a-t," ask your child what sound they hear first and last; your child should say "c" and "t"; make sure your child pronounces the correct letter sounds.

Step 3. Eye Training – Begin with this book. This book teaches the Alphabet letter sounds in picture form (m, a, n, r, f, s, e, t, l, g, c, k, b, i, h, d, p, o, j, w, u, v, q, x, y and z); then vowels and blended consonants (digraphs); you are teaching the letter sounds (phonemes) and not the words.

NOTE: The order in which the phonogram letter sounds are presented is based on the ease with which they are blended and able to be sounded out by children; it is not necessary for children to learn the letters in alphabetical order, or the names (long sound of the letters), as it may be confusing to learn the sounds and names of a letter at the same time.

With early readers it is best to keep things simple and step by step; for 2 and 3-year-old preschoolers keep lessons to one letter sound at a time and for a few minutes only; for 3 to 5 year old's this can be increased to 5 or 10 minutes; for fun, play based ways to teach your child to read see the book "Play Based Ways To Teach Your Child To Read" at http://howtoteachchildrentoread.ca

Step 4. Word Building vowels and consonants - Once your child can say all the short alphabet letter sounds go to the vowels and show how two consonants and a vowel create words; you could also teach the letter name or long sound of alphabet letters at this time.

Step 5. Word Building Digraphs - Digraphs are 2 or more letters forming one sound (a phoneme). Once a child has mastered the 26 Alphabet letter sounds, they are able to read most three letter words; once they master the most common letter blends (digraphs) they should be able to read most English written words.

TEACH YOUR PRE-SCHOOL CHILD TO READ METHOD

Point to the first letter sound in the first picture word and say "m".

Point to the first letter of the picture and ask, "What letter sound is this?"

If your child answers "m" correctly, point to the picture and say "mug".

THE LETTER "m"

mat
mop
mug

Point to the first letter sound in the first picture word and say "m" (all letters are lowercase short sound).

Point to the first letter of the picture and ask, "What letter sound is this?" If your child answers "m" correctly, point to the picture and say "mat".

Point to the first letter sound in the second picture word and say "m" (all letters are lowercase short sound).

Point to the first letter of the second picture and ask, "What letter sound is this?" If your child answers "m" correctly, point to the picture and say "mop".

Repeat the same process for the word "mug".

Your child should now recognize the letter sound "m".

Note: You are only teaching the first letter sound and not sounding or writing out the whole word.

All letters are lowercase or short letter sounds; we introduce capital long letter sounds and punctuation in other books by the author.

m_ _

m_ _

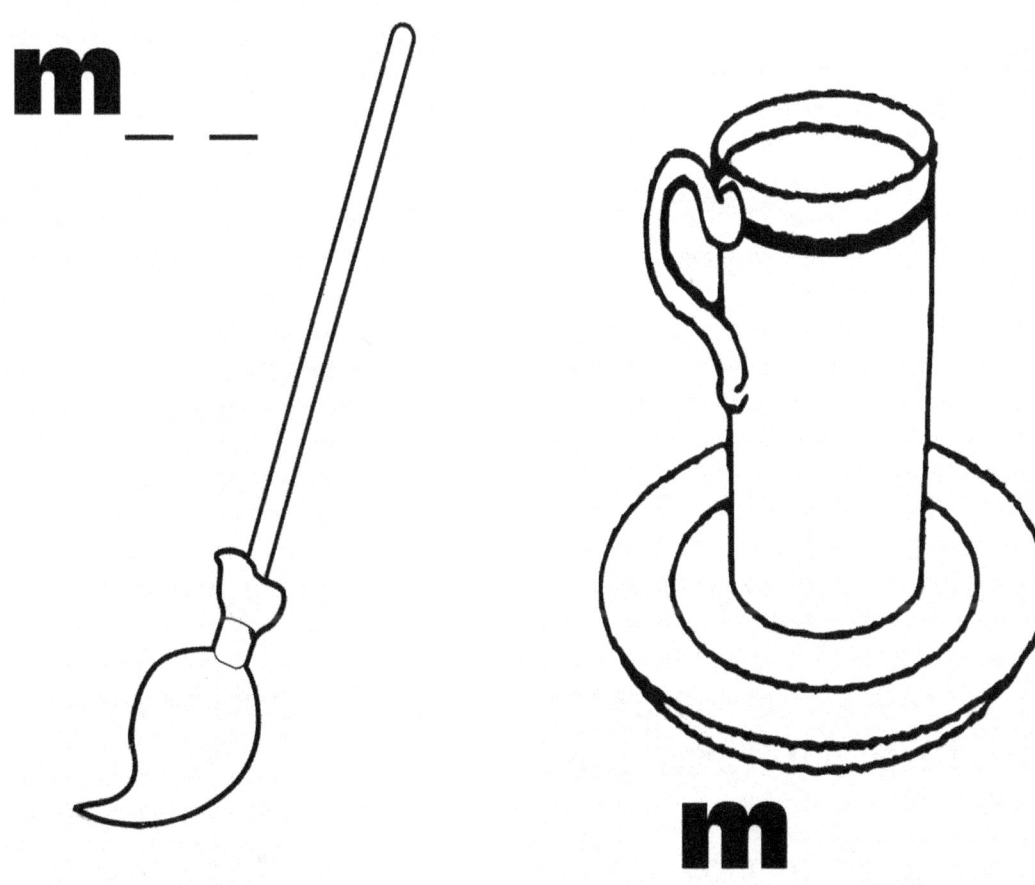

m_ _

THE LETTER "a"

ant

axe

apple

Point to the first letter sound in the first picture word and say "a" (all letters are lowercase short sound).

Point to the first letter of the picture and ask, "What letter sound is this?" If your child answers "a" correctly, point to the picture and say "ant".

Point to the first letter sound in the second picture word and say "a" (all letters are lowercase short sound).

Point to the first letter of the second picture and ask, "What letter sound is this?" If your child answers "a" correctly, point to the picture and say "axe".

Repeat the same process for the word "apple".

Note: You are only teaching the first letter sound and not sounding out the whole word.

Your child should now recognize the letter sound "a".

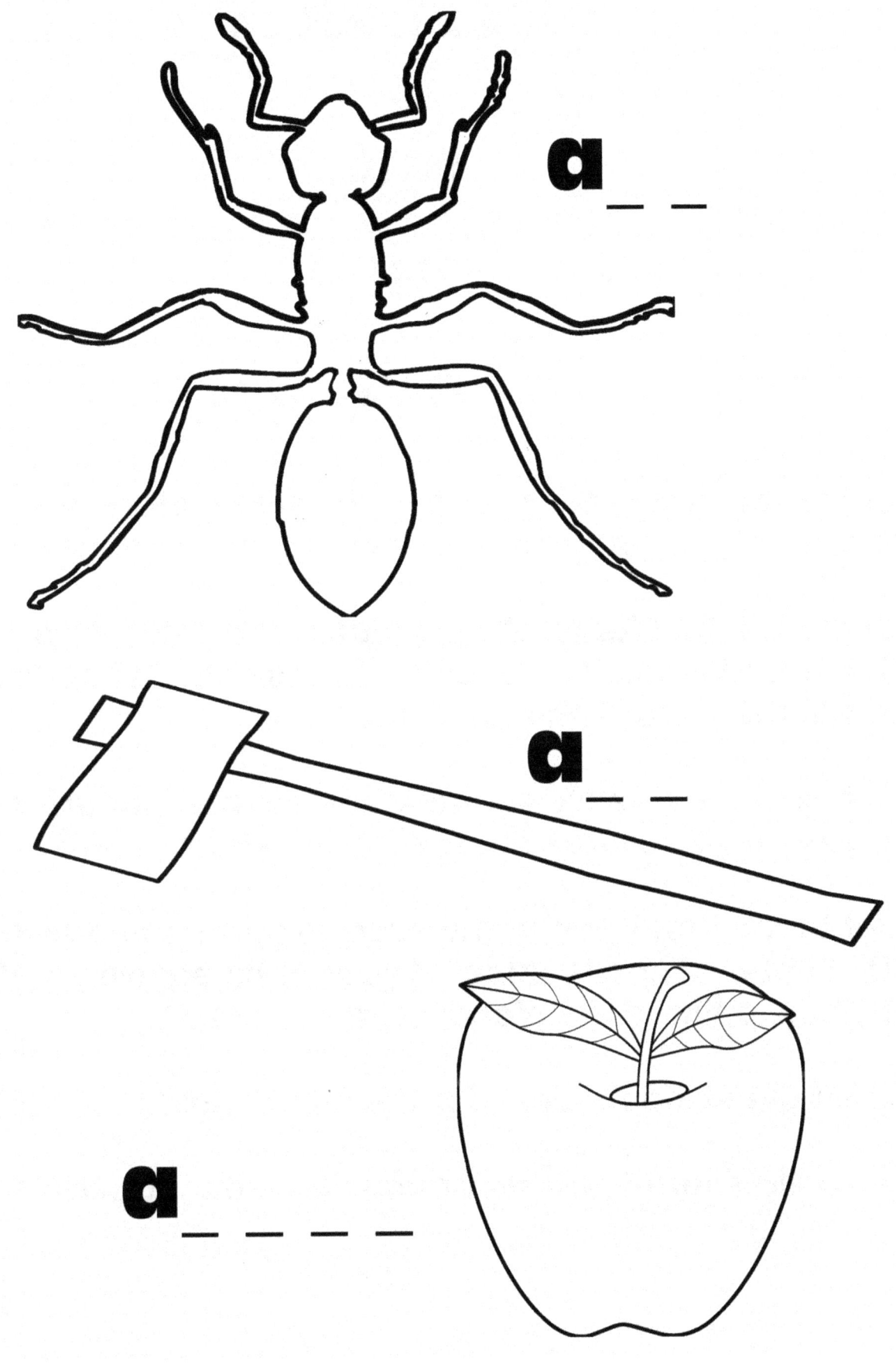

a _ _

a _ _

a _ _ _

THE LETTER "n"

nut

nun

net

Point to the first letter sound in the first picture word and say "n" (all letters are lowercase short sound).

Point to the first letter of the picture and ask, "What letter sound is this?" If your child answers "n" correctly, point to the picture and say "nut".

Point to the first letter sound in the second picture word and say "n" (all letters are lowercase short sound).

Point to the first letter of the second picture and ask, "What letter sound is this?" If your child answers "n" correctly, point to the picture and say "nun".

Repeat the same process for the word "net".

Your child should now recognize the letter sound "n".

THE LETTERS "m" "a" "n"

"m"
"a"
"n"

Point to each picture letter and have your child sound out each letter.

Ask your child to say the word; your child should say the word "man".

Let your child know that letter sounds make words and that words help us learn.

Note: preschool children may sound words out slowly; as they improve, point to the letters more quickly, so the child can say the whole word.

Note: from this point on all words that can be made from the letter sounds learned will be listed as "NEW WORDS."

NEW WORD: man.

THE LETTER "r"

rat
rod

Point to the first letter sound in the first picture word and say "r" (all letters are lowercase short sound).

Point to the first letter of the picture and ask, "What letter sound is this?" If your child answers "r" correctly, point to the picture and say "rat".

Point to the first letter sound in the second picture word and say "r" (all letters are lowercase short sound).

Point to the first letter of the second picture and ask, "What letter sound is this?" If your child answers "r" correctly, point to the picture and say "rod".

Your child should now recognize the letter sound "r".

NEW WORDS: ram, ran.

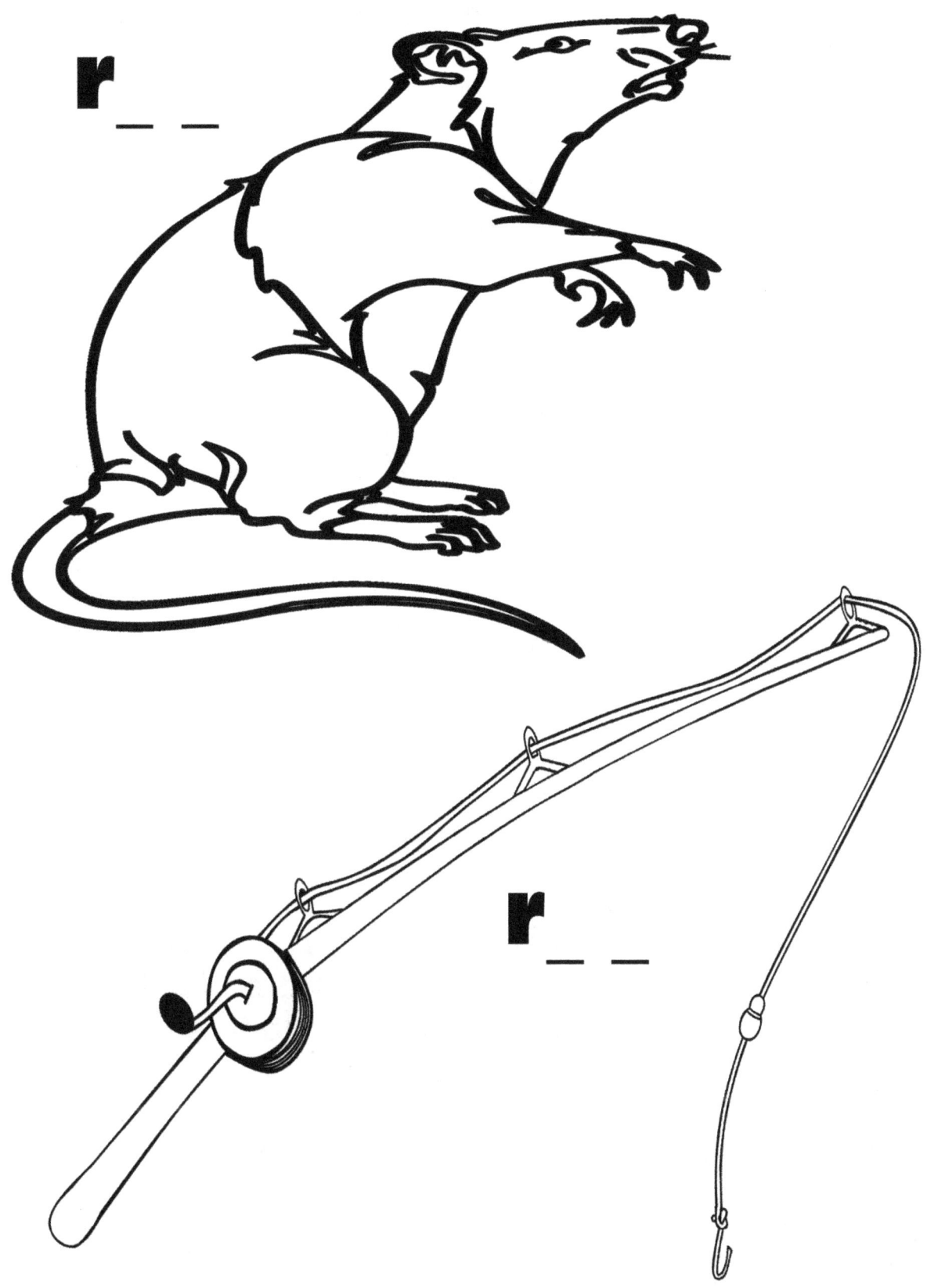

THE LETTERS "m" "a" "n" "r"

ram
ran
man

Point to the first letter "r" in the first picture, ask your child, "What letter sound is this?" Your child should answer "r".

Point to the second letter sound "a" of the first picture and ask, "What letter sound is this?" Your child should answer "a".

Point to the third letter sound "m" of the first picture and ask, "What letter sound is this?" Your child should answer "m".

Ask your child, "What word is this?" If your child cannot say the word, point to each letter sound and ask them to sound out each letter; speed up pointing to each letter until your child can say and recognize the word.

Repeat the same process for the words "ran" and "man".
Your child should now be able to sound out and say the words "ram", "ran" and "man".

ram

ran

man

THE LETTER "f"

fan

fig

fox

Point to the first letter sound in the first picture word and say "f" (all letters are lowercase short sound).

Point to the first letter of the picture and ask, "What letter sound is this?" If your child answers "f" correctly, point to the picture and say "fan".

Point to the first letter sound in the second picture word and say "f" (all letters are lowercase short sound).

Point to the first letter of the second picture and ask, "What letter sound is this?" If your child answers "f" correctly, point to the picture and say "fig".

Repeat process for the word "fox".

Your child should now recognize the letter sound "f".

NEW WORD: fan.

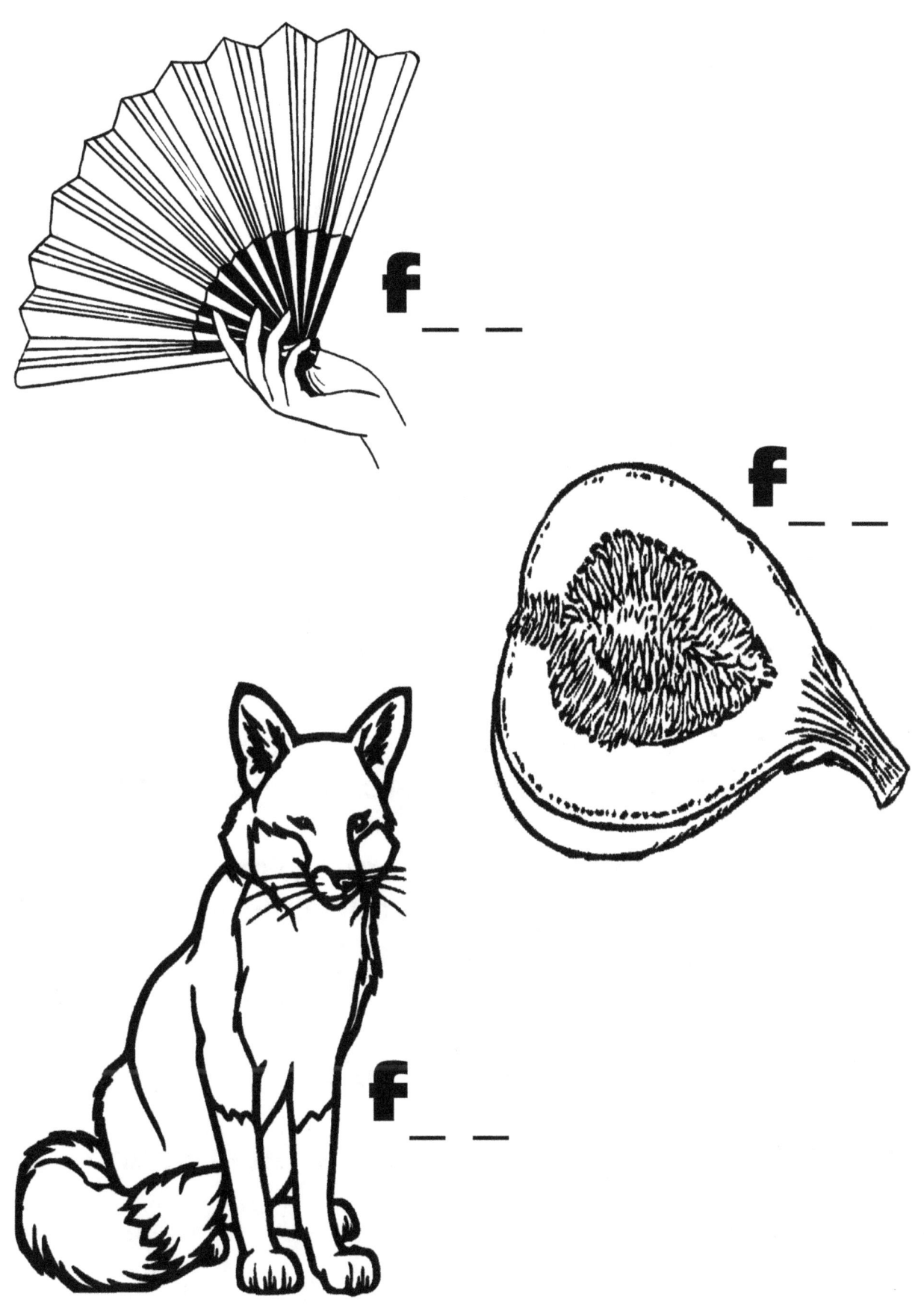

THE LETTER "s"

sun
six
sub

Point to the first letter sound in the first picture word and say "s" (all letters are lowercase short sound).

Point to the first letter of the picture and ask, "What letter sound is this?" If your child answers "s" correctly, point to the picture and say "sun".

Point to the first letter sound in the second picture word and say "s" (all letters are lowercase short sound).

Point to the first letter of the second picture and ask, "What letter sound is this?" If your child answers "s" correctly, point to the picture and say "six"; let your child know that there are six rabbits; count the rabbits.

Repeat process for the word "sub".

Your child should now recognize the letter sound "s".

NEW WORD: sam.

s _ _

s _ _

s _ _

THE LETTER "e"

egg
elf
elk

Point to the first letter sound in the first picture word and say "e" (all letters are lowercase short sound).

Point to the first letter of the picture and ask, "What letter sound is this?" If your child answers "e" correctly, point to the picture and say "egg".

Point to the first letter sound in the second picture word and say "e" (all letters are lowercase short sound).

Point to the first letter of the second picture and ask, "What letter sound is this?" If your child answers "e" correctly, point to the picture and say "elf".

Repeat process for the word "elk".

Your child should now recognize the letter sound "e".

NEW WORD: men.

e_ _

e_ _

e_ _

23

THE LETTERS "m" "a" "n" "r" "f" "s" "e"

man

men

ram

fan

sam

ran

Point to the first letter sound in the first picture word, say "m", then "a", then "n"; ask your child to say the word.

Point to the first letter sound of the second picture and ask, "What letter sound is this?"
Ask your child to sound out the letters and say the word.

Repeat the same process for all the letters and words.

Your child should now recognize the words man, men, ram, fan, sam and ran.

Note: if your child is unable to complete a step in the process, then you can sound out the letter for them or go back to the letter they are having difficulty with.

THE LETTER "t"

tub
tin
tap

Point to the first letter sound in the first picture word and say "t" (all letters are lowercase short sound).

Point to the first letter of the picture and ask, "What letter sound is this?" If your child answers "t" correctly, point to the picture and say "tub".

Point to the first letter sound in the second picture word and say "t" (all letters are lowercase short sound).

Point to the first letter of the second picture and ask, "What letter sound is this?" If your child answers "t" correctly, point to the picture and say "tin".

Repeat process for the word "tap".

Your child should now recognize the letter sound "t".

NEW WORDS: mat, met, nat, net, set, sat, rat, fat, ten, tan.

Note: give your child lots of praise and encouragement; if your child is not succeeding, then go back to the last lesson they were successful at.

t_ _

t_ _

t_ _

LETTER REVISION PRACTICE

Your child should be able to sound out the following words: men, man, fan, sam, ran, mat, met, nat, net, set, sat, rat, fat, ten, tan.

Point to the first letter of the first word and ask, "What letter sound is this?"

Ask your child to sound out each letter and say the word.

Repeat the same process for all the words; do not say the full word, only the first lowercase short letter sound of each word; and only help where necessary.

Your child should now recognize the letter sounds "m" "a" "n" "r" "f" "s" "e" "t".

Note: at this point we are not capitalizing names or adding punctuation; all words will be lowercase or short letter sounds.

men	man
fan	sam
ran	mat
met	nat
net	set
sat	rat
fat	ten
tan	

THE LETTER "l"

lab

leg

lid

log

Point to the first letter sound in the first picture word and say "l" (all letters are lowercase short sound).

Point to the first letter of the picture and ask, "What letter sound is this?" If your child answers "l" correctly, point to the picture and say "lab".

Point to the first letter sound in the second picture word and say "l" (all letters are lowercase short sound).

Point to the first letter of the second picture and ask, "What letter sound is this?" If your child answers "l" correctly, point to the picture and say "leg".

Repeat process for the word "lid" and "log".

Your child should now recognize the letter sound "l".

NEW WORDS: let.

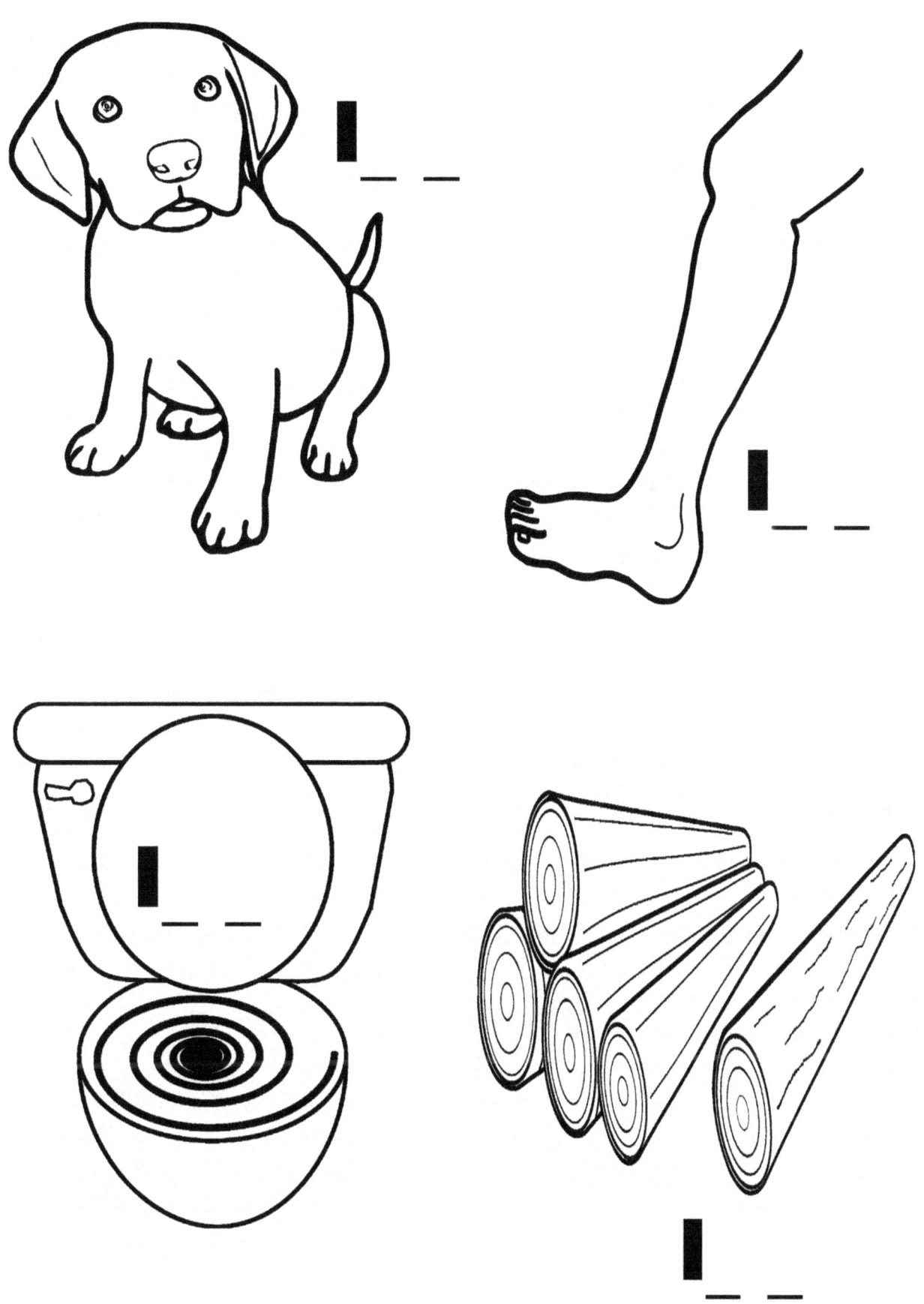

THE LETTER "g"

gas
gun

Point to the first letter sound in the first picture word and say "g" (all letters are lowercase short sound).

Point to the first letter of the picture and ask, "What letter sound is this?" If your child answers "g" correctly, point to the picture and say "gas".

Point to the first letter sound in the second picture word and say "g" (all letters are lowercase short sound).

Point to the first letter of the second picture and ask, "What letter sound is this?" If your child answers "g" correctly, point to the picture and say "gun".

Your child should now recognize the letter sound "g".

NEW WORDS: rag, tag, sag, gas, get, gag.

g_ _

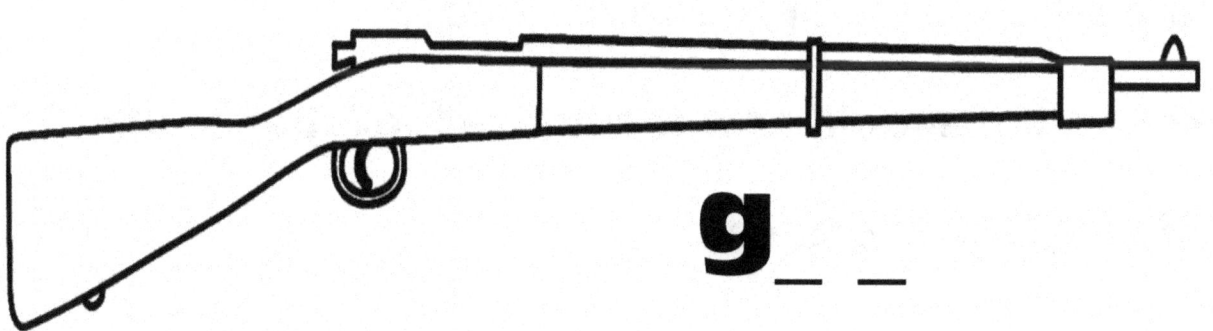

g_ _

THE LETTER "c"

cat
cup
cop

Point to the first letter sound in the first picture word and say "c" (all letters are lowercase short sound).

Point to the first letter of the picture and ask, "What letter sound is this?" If your child answers "c" correctly, point to the picture and say "cat".

Point to the first letter sound in the second picture word and say "c" (all letters are lowercase short sound).

Point to the first letter of the second picture and ask, "What letter sound is this?" If your child answers "c" correctly, point to the picture and say "cup".

Repeat process for the word "cop".

Your child should now recognize the letter sound "c".

NEW WORDS: cat, can.

c_ _

c_ _

c_ _

THE LETTER "k"

keg
kid

Point to the first letter sound in the first picture word and say "k" (all letters are lowercase short sound).

Point to the first letter of the picture and ask, "What letter sound is this?" If your child answers correctly "k", point to the picture and say "keg".

Point to the first letter sound in the second picture word and say "k" (all letters are lowercase short sound).

Point to the first letter of the second picture and ask, "What letter sound is this?" If your child answers "k" correctly, point to the picture and say "kid".

Your child should now recognize the letter sound "k".

NEW WORDS: keg.

Note: let your child know that "c" and "k" have the same sound, but the written letters are different.

k _ _

k _ _

THE LETTER "b"

bag
bat

Point to the first letter sound in the first picture word and say "b" (all letters are lowercase short sound).

Point to the first letter of the picture and ask, "What letter sound is this?" If your child answers "b" correctly, point to the picture and say "bag".

Point to the first letter sound in the second picture word and say "b" (all letters are lowercase short sound).

Point to the first letter of the second picture and ask, "What letter sound is this?" If your child answers "b" correctly, point to the picture and say "bat".

Your child should now recognize the letter sound "b".

NEW WORDS: cab, tab, ben, bat, bag, beg.

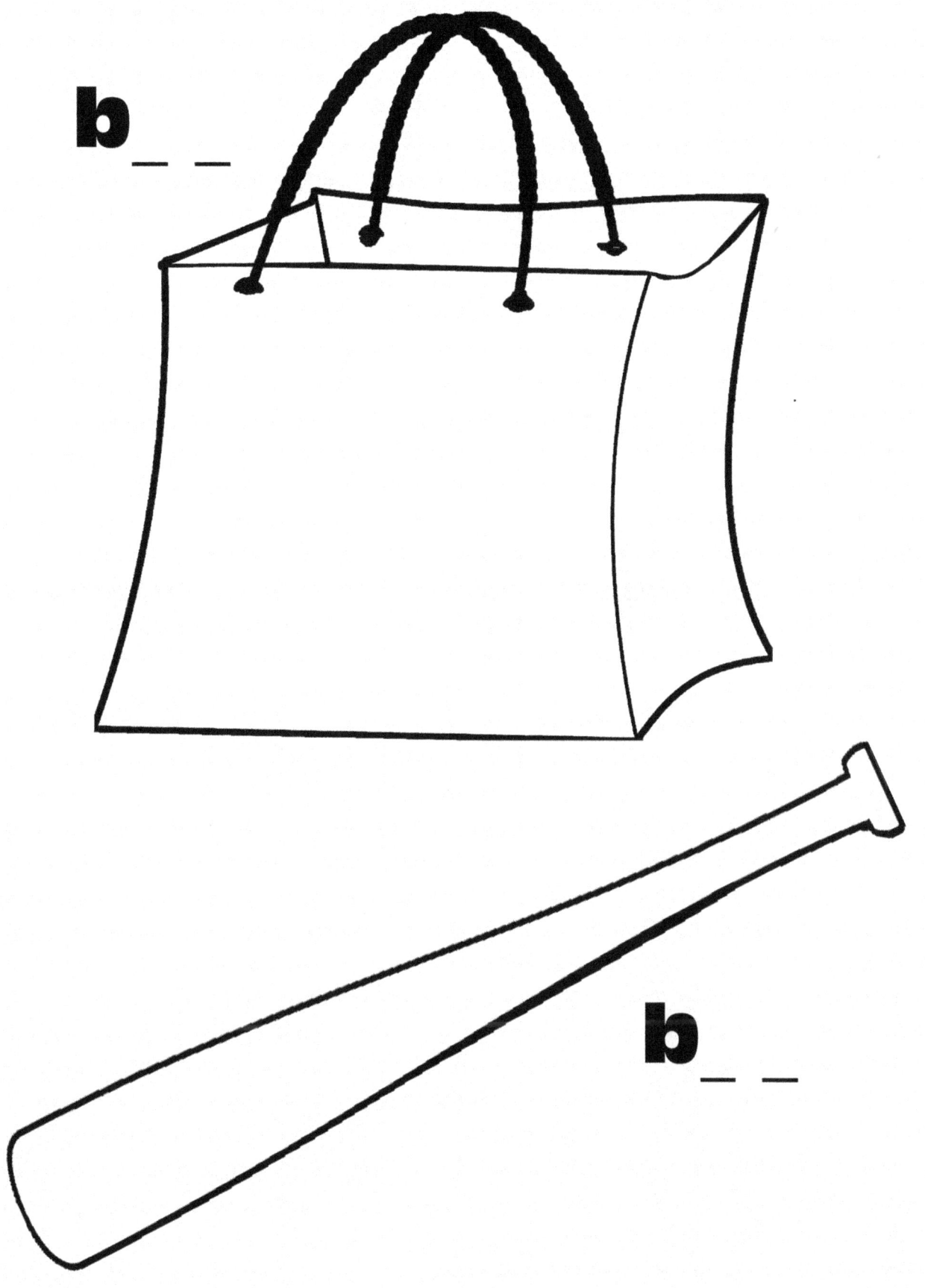

LETTER REVISION PRACTICE

Your child should be able to sound out the following words: men, man, fan, sam, ran, mat, met, nat, net, set, sat, rat, fat, ten, tan, let, rag, tag, sag, gas, get, gag, cat, can, keg, cab, tab, ben, bat, bag, beg.

Point to the first letter of the first word and ask, "What letter sound is this?"

Ask your child to sound out each letter and say the word.

Repeat the same process for all the words; do not say the full word, only the first lowercase short letter sound of each word; and only help where necessary.

Your child should now recognize the letter sounds "m" "a" "n" "r" "f" "s" "e" "t" "l" "g" "c" "k" "b".

men	man	fan
sam	ran	mat
met	nat	net
set	sat	rat
fat	ten	tan
let	rag	tag
sag	gas	get
gag	cat	can
keg	cab	tab
ben	bat	bag
beg		

THE LETTER "i"

ink
inch

Point to the first letter sound in the first picture word and say "i" (all letters are lowercase short sound).

Point to the first letter of the picture and ask, "What letter sound is this?" If your child answers "i" correctly, point to the picture and say "ink".

Point to the first letter sound in the second picture word and say "i" (all letters are lowercase short sound).

Point to the first letter of the second picture and ask, "What letter sound is this?" If your child answers "i" correctly, point to the picture and say "inch".

Your child should now recognize the letter sound "i".

NEW WORDS: bit, sit, fig, tin, fit, rib, bib, big, fin, rim.

i_ _

i_ _ _

THE LETTER "h"

hat

hen

Point to the first letter sound in the first picture word and say "h" (all letters are lowercase short sound).

Point to the first letter of the picture and ask, "What letter sound is this?" If your child answers "h" correctly, point to the picture and say "hat".

Point to the first letter sound in the second picture word and say "h" (all letters are lowercase short sound).

Point to the first letter of the second picture and ask, "What letter sound is this?" If your child answers "h" correctly, point to the picture and say "hen".

Your child should now recognize the letter sound "h".

NEW WORDS: hat, hit, hem, ham, him, hen.

h _ _

h _ _

THE LETTER "d"

dog
dig

Point to the first letter sound in the first picture word and say "d".

Point to the first letter of the picture and ask, "What letter sound is this?" If your child answers "d" correctly, point to the picture and say "dog".

Point to the first letter sound in the second picture word and say "d" (all letters are lowercase short sound).

Point to the first letter of the second picture and ask, "What letter sound is this?" If your child answers "d" correctly, point to the picture and say "dig".

Your child should now recognize the letter sound "d".

NEW WORDS: red, rid, lad, led, lid, fed, hid, had, mad, mid, bed, bad, sad, did, den, dip, dig, dim.

d _ _

d _ _

LETTER REVISION PRACTICE

Your child should be able to sound out the following words: bit, sit, fig, tin, fit, rib, bib, big, fin, rim, hat, hit, hem, ham, him, hen, red, rid, lad, led, lid, fed, hid, had, mad, mid, bed, bad, sad, did, den, dip, dig, dim.

Point to the first letter of the first word and ask, "What letter sound is this?"

Ask your child to sound out each letter and say the word.

Repeat the same process for all the words; do not say the full word, only the first lowercase short letter sound of each word; and only help where necessary.

Your child should now recognize the letter sounds: "m" "a" "n" "r" "f" "s" "e" "t" "l" "g" "c" "k" "b" "i" "h" "d".

bit	sit	fig
tin	fit	rib
bib	big	fin
rim	hat	hit
hem	ham	him
hen	red	rid
lad	led	lid
fed	hid	had
mad	mid	bed
bad	sad	did
den	dip	dig
dim		

THE LETTER "p"

pan

peg

pin

Point to the first letter sound in the first picture word and say "p".

Point to the first letter of the picture and ask, "What letter sound is this?" If your child answers "p" correctly, point to the picture and say "pan".

Point to the first letter sound in the second picture word and say "p" (all letters are lowercase short sound).

Point to the first letter of the second picture and ask, "What letter sound is this?" If your child answers "p" correctly, point to the picture and say "peg".

Repeat process for the word "pin".

Your child should now recognize the letter sound "p".

NEW WORDS: tap tip rip rap sip sap nap map lap lip cap dip hip pan pin pen pet pat pit pig peg.

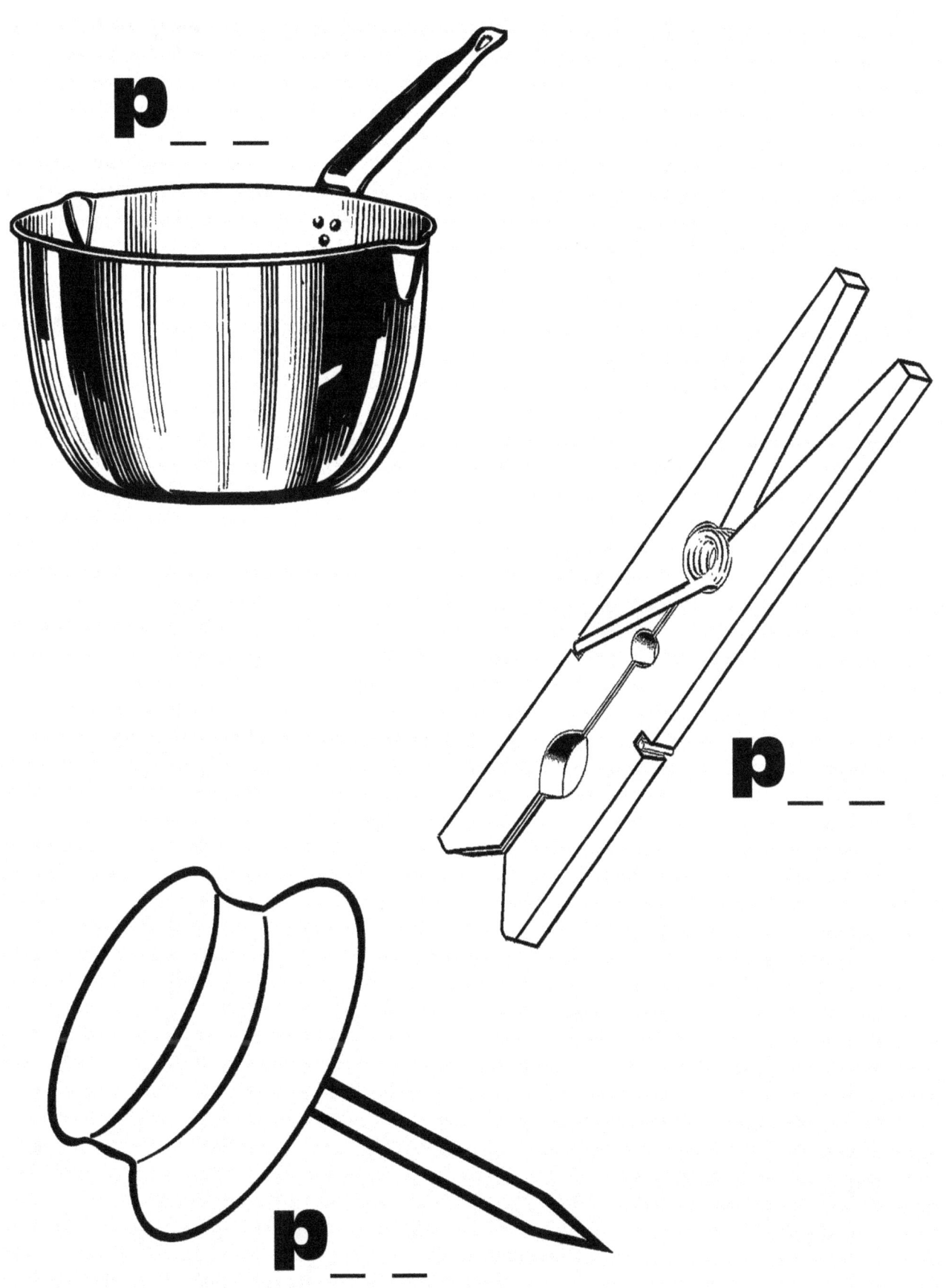

LETTER REVISION PRACTICE

Your child should be able to sound out the following words: tap tip rip rap sip sap nap map lap lip cap dip hip pan pin pen pet pat pit pig peg.

Point to the first letter of the first word and ask, "What letter sound is this?"

Ask your child to sound out each letter and say the word.

Repeat the same process for all the words; do not say the full word, only the first lowercase short letter sound of each word; and only help where necessary.

Your child should now recognize the letter sounds: "m" "a" "n" "r" "f" "s" "e" "t" "l" "g" "c" "k" "b" "i" "h" "d" "p".

tap	tip	rip
rap	sip	sap
nap	map	lap
lip	cap	dip
hip	pan	pin
pen	pet	pat
pit	pig	peg

THE LETTER "o"

ox

otter

Point to the first letter sound in the first picture word and say "o".

Point to the first letter of the picture and ask, "What letter sound is this?" If your child answers "o" correctly, point to the picture and say "ox".

Point to the first letter sound in the second picture word and say "o" (all letters are lowercase short sound).

Point to the first letter of the second picture and ask, "What letter sound is this?" If your child answers "o" correctly, point to the picture and say "otter".

Your child should now recognize the letter sound "o".

NEW WORDS: log, fog, cob, rob, nod, sod, pod, rod, hop, top, got, pot, hot, lot, dot.

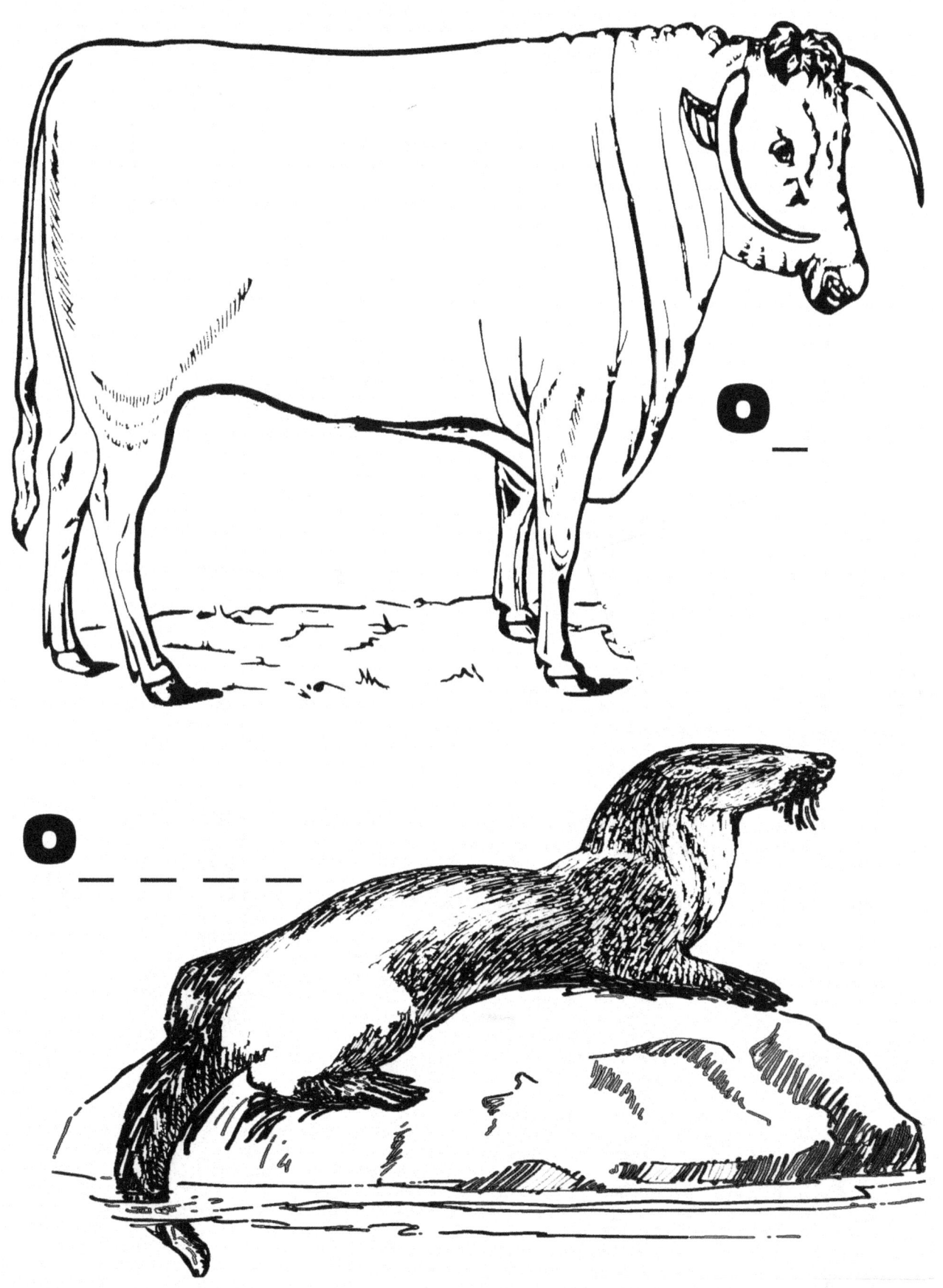

o_

o_ _ _ _

THE LETTER "j"

jam

jet

Point to the first letter sound in the first picture word and say "j".

Point to the first letter of the picture and ask, "What letter sound is this?" If your child answers "j" correctly, point to the picture and say "jam".

Point to the first letter sound in the second picture word and say "j" (all letters are lowercase short sound).

Point to the first letter of the second picture and ask, "What letter sound is this?" If your child answers "j" correctly, point to the picture and say "jet".

Your child should now recognize the letter sound "j".

NEW WORDS: jam, jet, jab, jig, jog, jot.

j_ _

j_ _

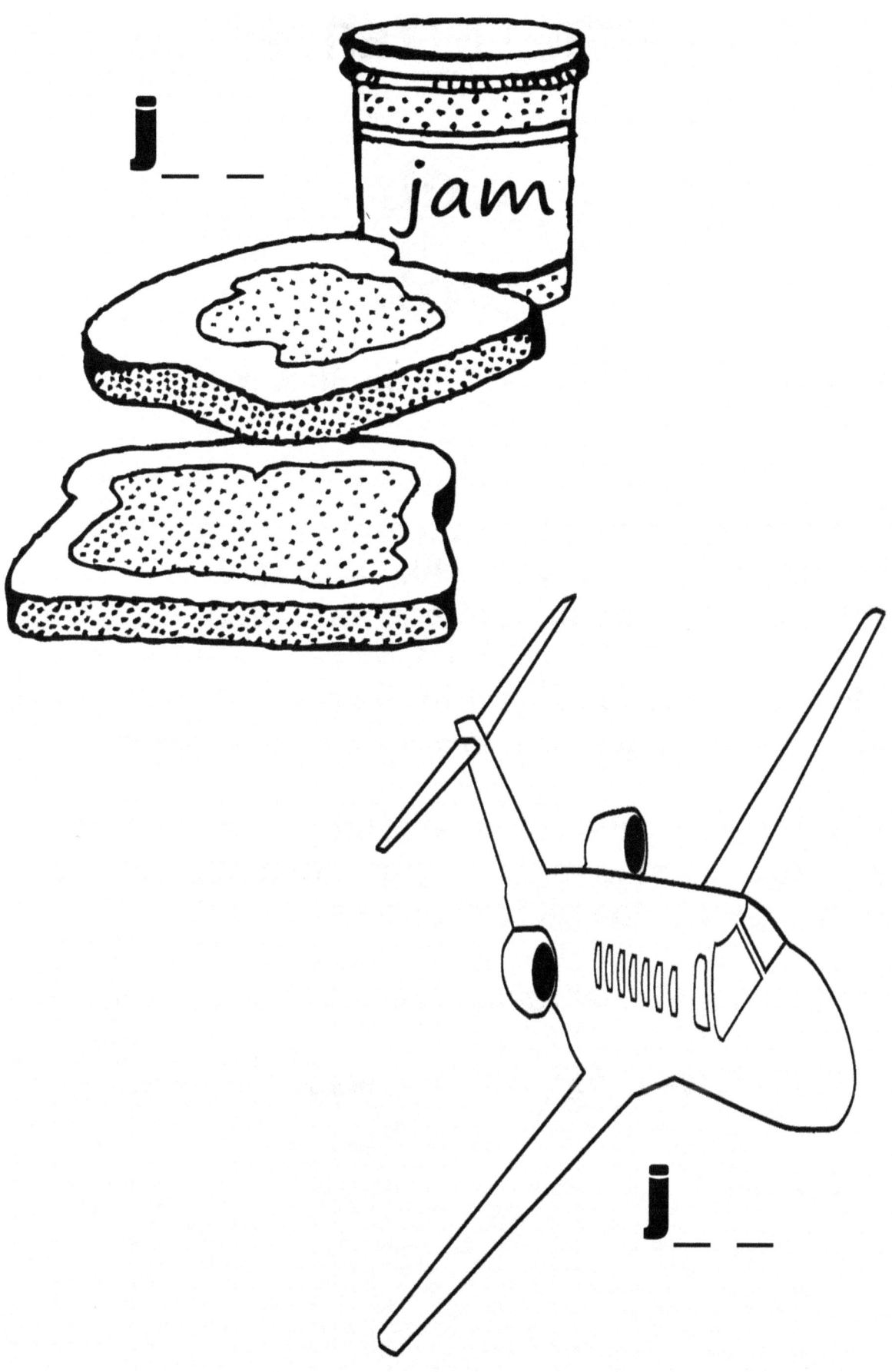

THE LETTER "w"

web

wok

Point to the first letter sound in the first picture word and say "w".

Point to the first letter of the picture and ask, "What letter sound is this?" If your child answers "w" correctly, point to the picture and say "web".

Point to the first letter sound in the second picture word and say "w" (all letters are lowercase short sound).

Point to the first letter of the second picture and ask, "What letter sound is this?" If your child answers "w" correctly, point to the picture and say "wok".

Your child should now recognize the letter sound "w".

NEW WORDS: wag, wig, wit, wet, web, win, wok.

w_ _

w_ _

LETTER REVISION PRACTICE

Your child should be able to sound out the following words: log, fog, cob, rob, nod, sod, pod, rod, hop, top, got, pot, hot, lot, dot, jam, jet, jab, jig, jog, jot, wag, wig, wit, wet, web, win, wok.

Point to the first letter of the first word and ask, "What letter sound is this?"

Ask your child to sound out and say the word.

Repeat the same process for all the words; do not say the full word, only the first lowercase short letter sound of each word; and only help where necessary.

Your child should now recognize the letter sounds: "m" "a" "n" "r" "f" "s" "e" "t" "l" "g" "c" "k" "b" "i" "h" "d" "p" "o" "j" "w".

log	fog	cob
rob	nod	sod
pod	rod	hop
top	got	pot
hot	lot	dot
jam	jet	jab
jig	jog	jot
wag	wig	wit
wet	web	win
wok		

THE LETTER "u"

up

umbrella

Point to the first letter sound in the first picture word and say "u".

Point to the first letter of the picture and ask, "What letter sound is this?" If your child answers "u" correctly, point to the picture and say "up".

Point to the first letter sound in the second picture word and say "u" (all letters are lowercase short sound).

Point to the first letter of the second picture and ask, "What letter sound is this?" If your child answers "u" correctly, point to the picture and say "umbrella".

Your child should now recognize the letter sound "u".

NEW WORDS: gum, hum, bug, rug, hug, jug, pug, tug, tub, hub, rub, mud, bud, sup, cup, pup, run, bun, fun, gun, sun, cut, hut, but, nut, us, up.

u_

u_ _ _ _ _ _ _ _

THE LETTER "v"

van

vet

Point to the first letter sound in the first picture word and say "v".

Point to the first letter of the picture and ask, "What letter sound is this?" If your child answers "v" correctly, point to the picture and say "van".

Point to the first letter sound in the second picture word and say "v" (all letters are lowercase short sound).

Point to the first letter of the second picture and ask, "What letter sound is this?" If your child answers "v" correctly, point to the picture and say "vet".

Your child should now recognize the letter sound "v".

NEW WORDS: van, vat, vet.

v _ _

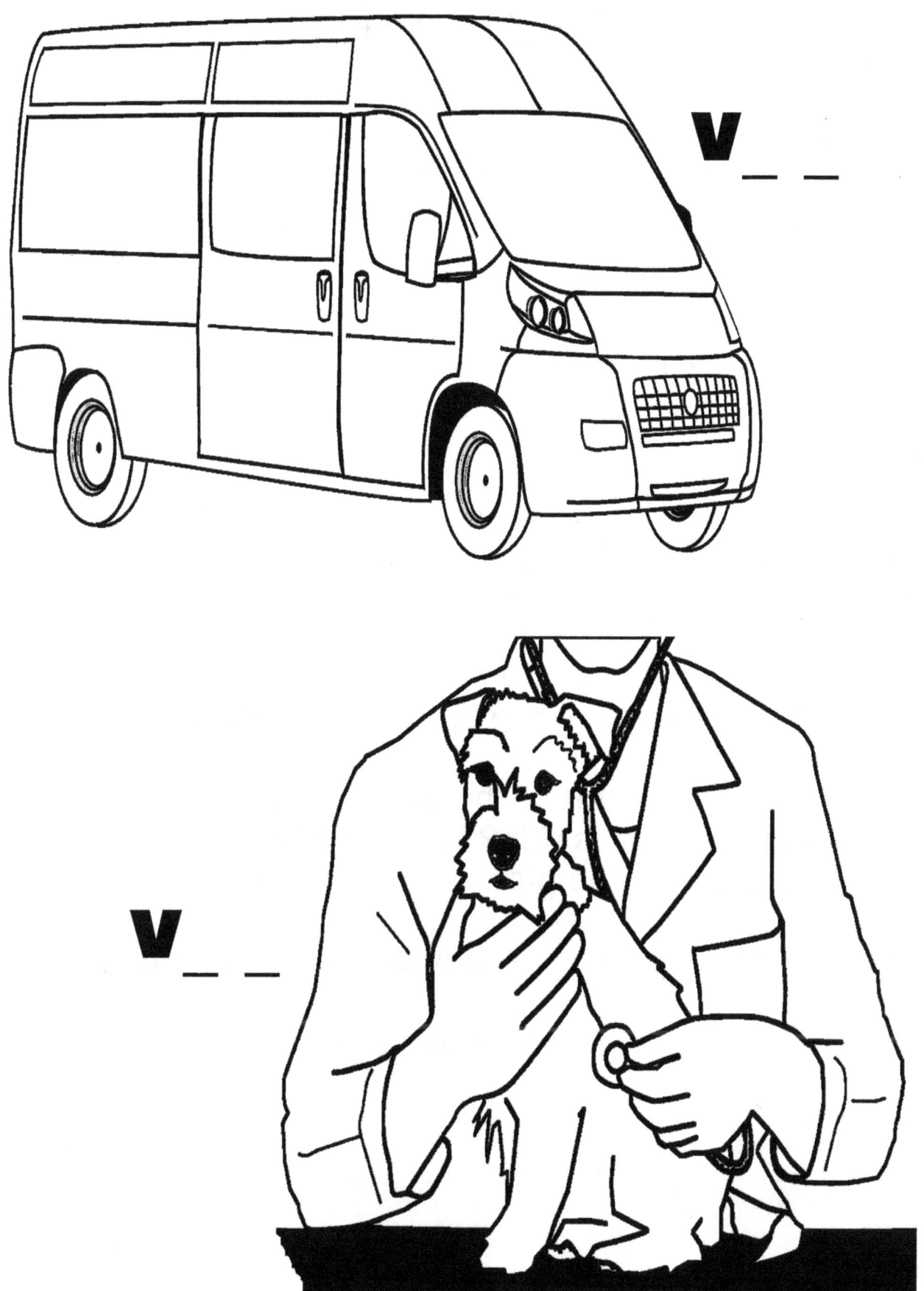

v _ _ _

THE LETTER "q"

queen
qat

Point to the first letter sound in the first picture word and say "q".

Point to the first letter of the picture and ask, "What letter sound is this?" If your child answers "q" correctly, point to the picture and say "queen".

Point to the first letter sound in the second picture word and say "q" (all letters are lowercase short sound).

Point to the first letter of the second picture and ask, "What letter sound is this?" If your child answers "q" correctly, point to the picture and say "qat".

Your child should now recognize the letter sound "q".

NEW WORDS: queen, qat, quit, quilt.

q _ _ _ _ _

q _ _

THE LETTER "x"

ax
mix

Point to the second letter sound in the first picture word and say "x".

Point to the second letter of the picture and ask, "What letter sound is this?" If your child answers "x" correctly, point to the picture and say "ax".

Point to the third letter sound in the second picture word and say "x" (all letters are lowercase short sound).

Point to the third letter of the second picture and ask, "What letter sound is this?" If your child answers "x" correctly, point to the picture and say "mix".

Your child should now recognize the letter sound "x".

NEW WORDS: ax, box, six, mix, vex.

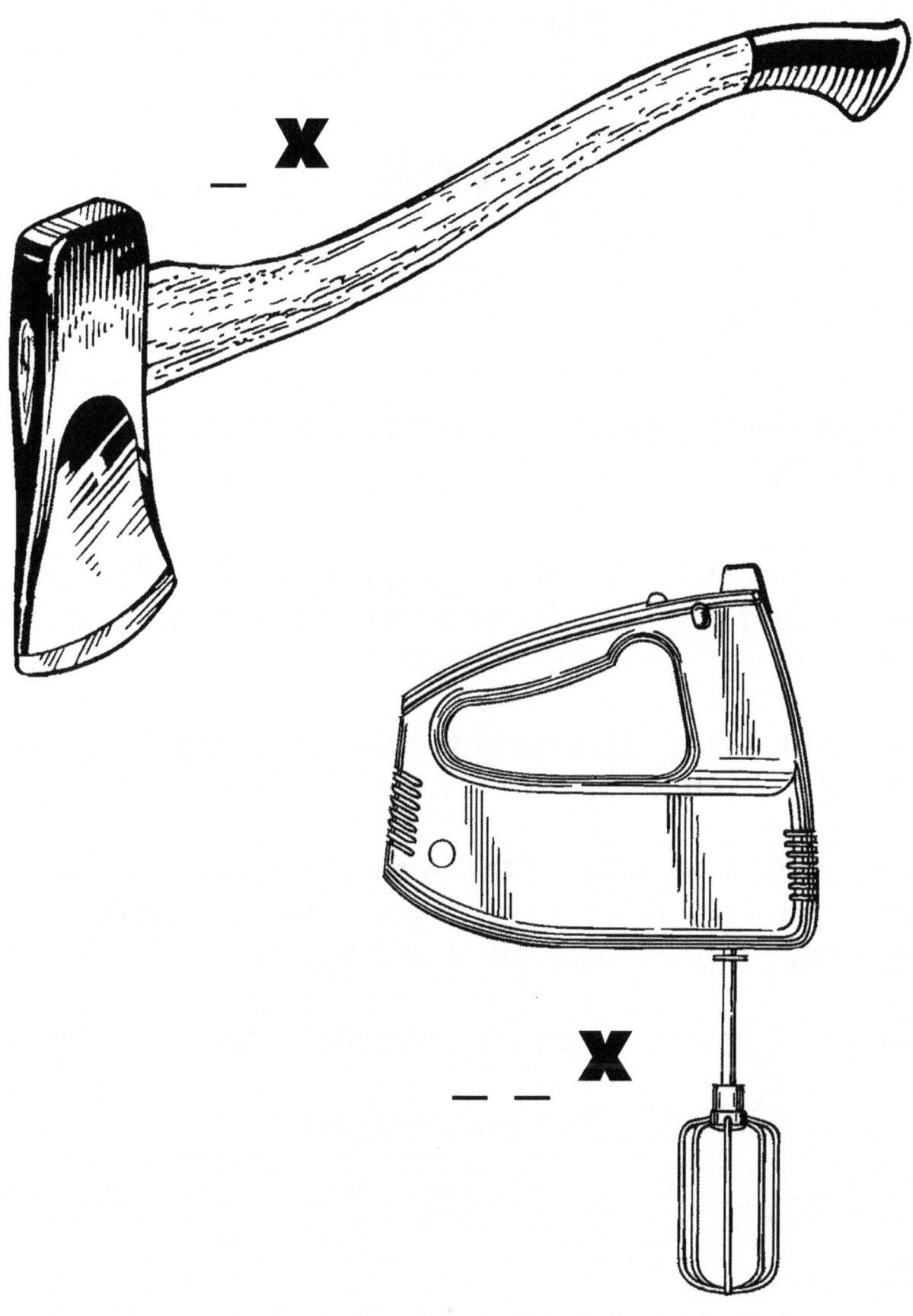

THE LETTER "y"

yak

yam

Point to the first letter sound in the first picture word and say "y".

Point to the first letter of the picture and ask, "What letter sound is this?" If your child answers "y" correctly, point to the picture and say "yak".

Point to the first letter sound in the second picture word and say "y" (all letters are lowercase short sound).

Point to the first letter of the second picture and ask, "What letter sound is this?" If your child answers "y" correctly, point to the picture and say "yam".

Your child should now recognize the letter sound "y".

NEW WORDS: yak, yam, yen, yes, yet.

y_ _

y_ _

THE LETTER "z"

zip

zebra

Point to the first letter sound in the first picture word and say lowercase (short) "z".

Point to the first letter of the picture and ask, "What letter sound is this?" If your child answers "z" correctly, point to the picture and say "zip".

Point to the first letter sound in the second picture word and say "z" (all letters are lowercase short sound).

Point to the first letter of the second picture and ask, "What letter sound is this?" If your child answers "z" correctly, point to the picture and say "zebra".

Your child should now recognize the letter sound "z".

NEW WORDS: zip, fez, zebra.

z _ _

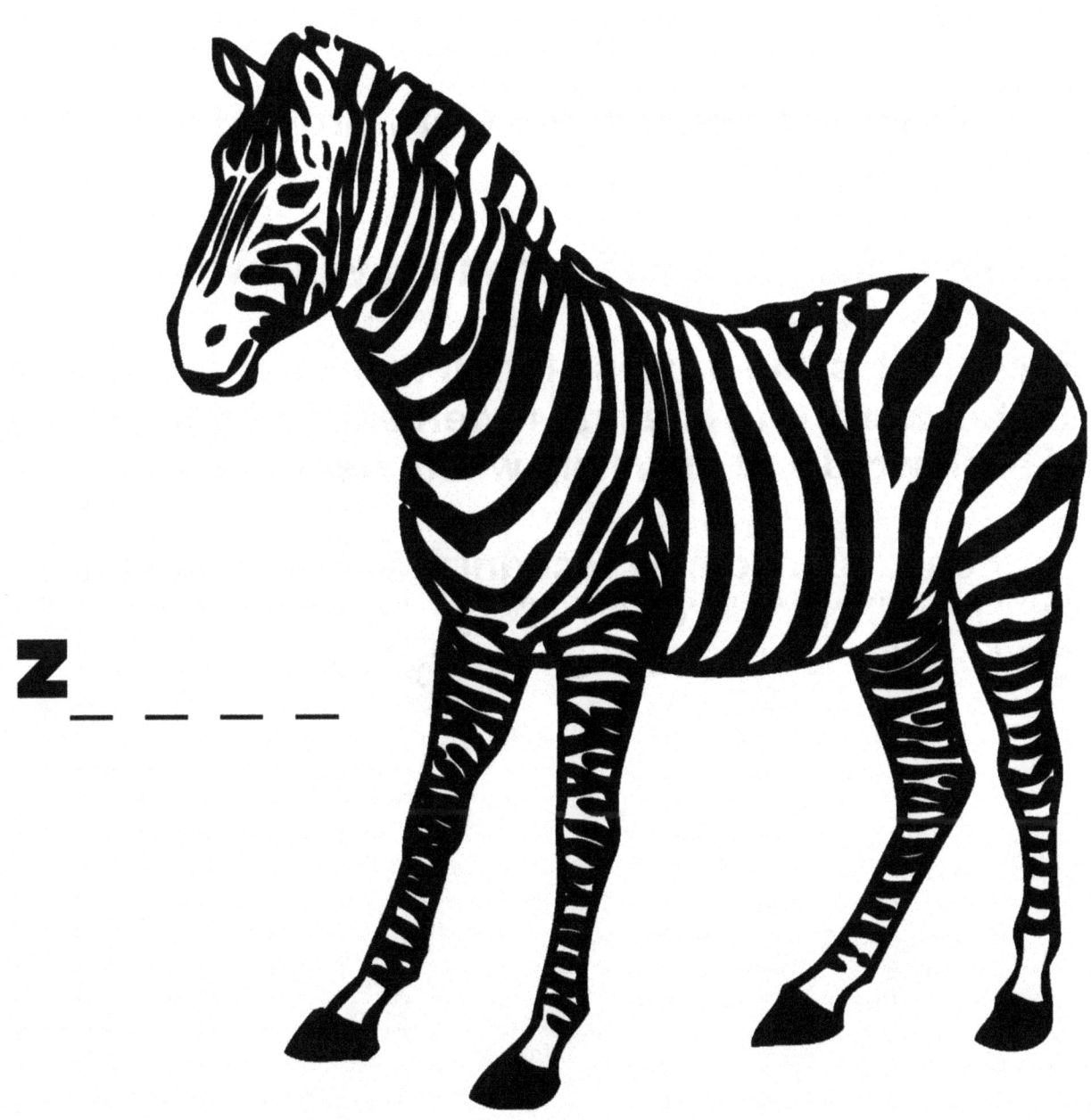

z _ _ _ _

LETTER REVISION PRACTICE

Your child should be able to sound out the following words: gum, hum, bug, rug, hug, jug, pug, tug, tub, hub, rub, mud, bud, sup, cup, pup, run, bun, fun, gun, sun, cut, hut, but, nut, us, up, van, vat, vet, queen, qat, quit, quilt, ax, box, six, mix, vex, yak, yam, yen, yes, yet, zip, fez, zebra.

Point to the first letter of the first word and ask, "What letter sound is this?"

Ask your child to sound out and say the word.

Repeat the same process for all the words; do not say the full word, only the first lowercase short letter sound of each word and only help where necessary.

Your child should now recognize the letter sounds: "m" "a" "n" "r" "f" "s" "e" "t" "l" "g" "c" "k" "b" "i" "h" "d" "p" "o" "j" "w" "u" "v" "q" "x" "y" "z".

gum hum bug rug
hug jug pug tug
tub hub rub mud
bud sup cup pup
run bun fun gun
sun cut hut but
nut us up van
vat vet queen qat
quit quilt ax box
six mix vex yak
yam yen yes yet
zip fez zebra

5 VOWEL SOUNDS

"a" as in "ant".
Phonic Rules: "a" has 5 sounds.

"e" as in "elk".
Phonic Rules: "e" has 2 sounds.

"i" as in "ink".
Phonic Rules: "i" has 2 sounds.

"o" as in "ox".
Phonic Rules: "o" has 4 sounds.

"u" as in "sun".
Phonic Rules: "u" has 3 sounds.

English Words: usually have a vowel with one, two, or more consonants (CVC) which make up most English language words.

Note: you are only teaching your child the one lowercase (short) vowel Alphabet letter sound at this time.

Do not teach the Phonic rules until your child can fully recognize the 50 blended consonants (digraph sounds).

a

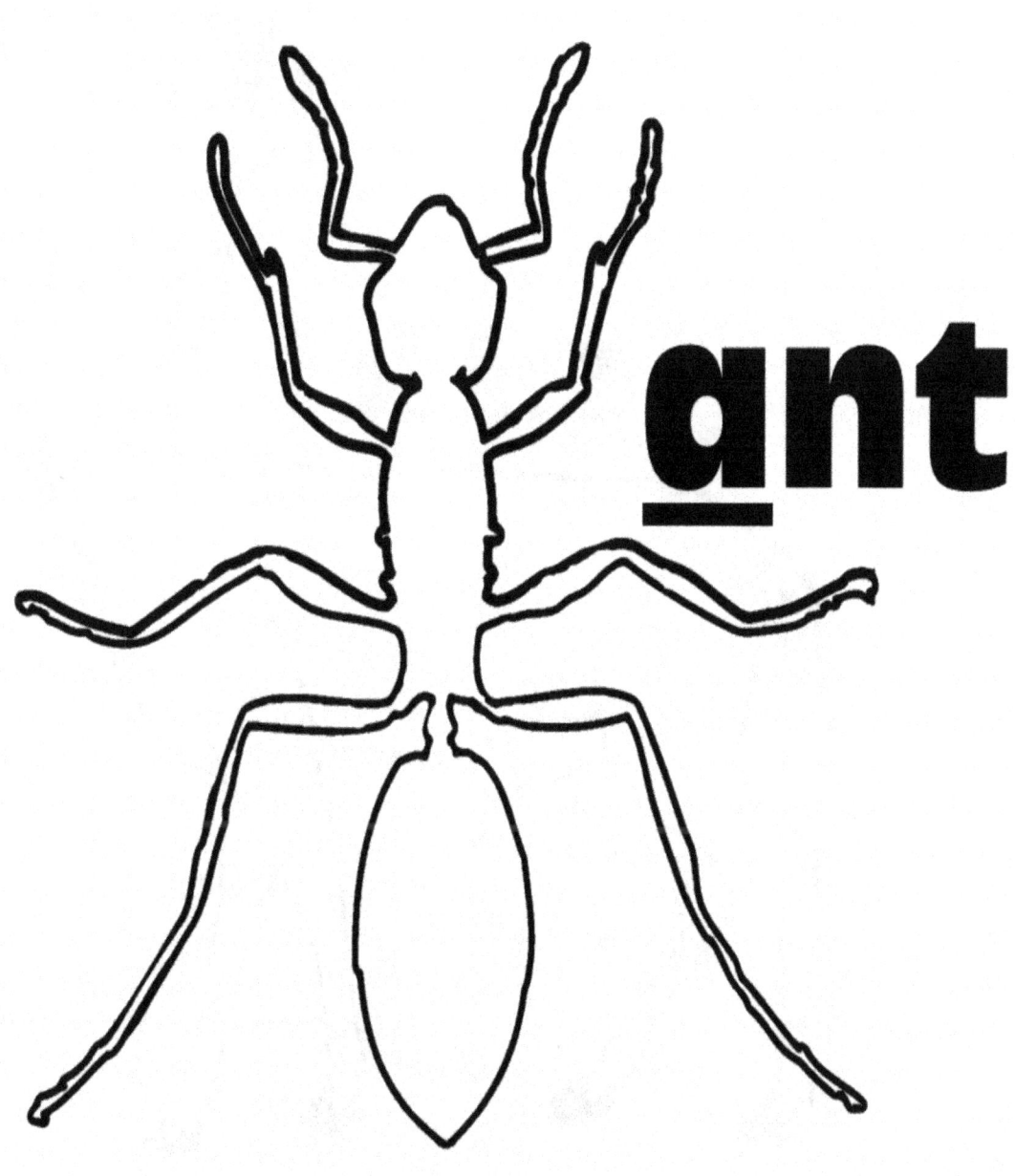

ant

e

elk

i

ink ink

o

ox

U

s__u__n__

VOWEL SOUNDS – "a" – "e" – "i" – "o" – "u"

Phonic rules:
The letter "a" has 5 sounds – apple – ball – cake – chair – yacht.

METHOD:
Point to the "a" in "apple" say "a".
Point to the "a" in "cake" say "A" (long "A").
Point to the "a" in "ball" say "a" ("aw" sound).
Point to the "a" in "chair" say "a" ("air" sound).
Point to the "a" in "yacht say "a" ("o" sound).

The letter "e" has 2 sounds – elephant – eagle.

The letter "i" has 2 sounds – insect – pie.

The letter "o" has 4 sounds – octopus – overcoat – oven – owl.

The letter "u" has 3 sounds – umbrella – urn – unicorn.

Let your child know that some letters have more than one sound.

Go slow; take your time, and make sure your child understands the lesson before you move on.

"e"

elephant

eagle

"i"

insect

pie

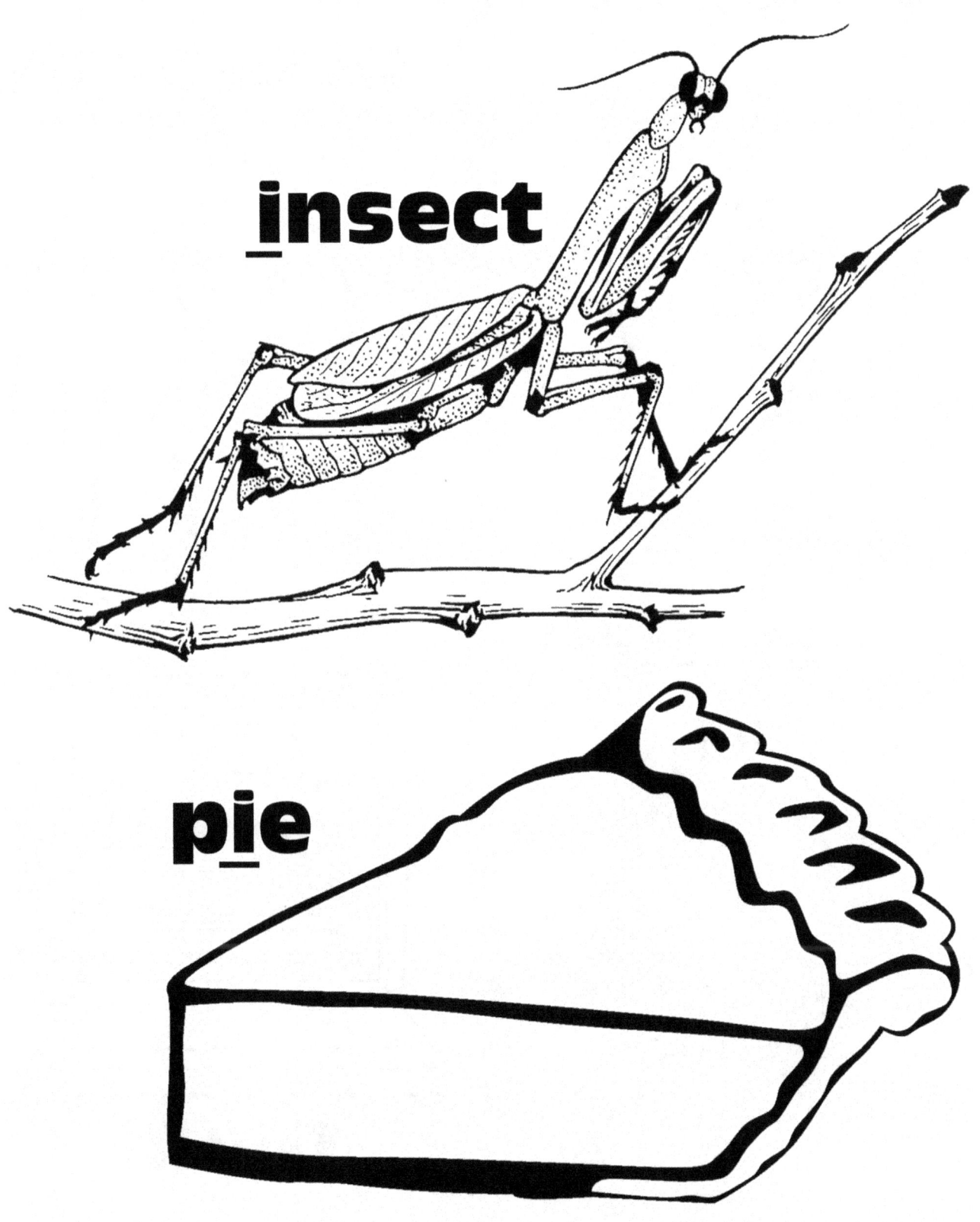

octopus "o"

overcoat

owl

oven

"U"

umbrella

unicorn

urn

SHORT AND LONG VOWELS

short and long vowel sounds "a"-"A"; "e"-"E"; "i"-"I"; "o"-"O"; "u"-"U".

Phonic Rules: When "*e*" is the last letter in a word, the first vowel usually says its name (long sound) and the *e* is silent.

SHORT VOWEL	LONG VOWEL
can	cane
tap	tape
met	meter
pin	pine
win	wine
din	dine
rip	ripe
bit	bite
rid	ride
mop	moped
rob	robe
hop	hope
not	note
rod	rode
cub	cube
tub	tube

NEW SOUND - "s" = "z"

Phonic Rules:
adding an "s" or "es" at the end of a word usually means there is more than one item.
"s" often has the sound of "z" (hose).

"s"
cat – cats
cup – cups
sit – sits
dip – dips
top – tops
rope – ropes

"z"
as – has
is – his
hose – hoses
rose – roses
fuse – fuses

Let your child know that some letters have more than one sound.

Go slow; take your time, and make sure your child understands the lesson before you move on.

cat  **cats**

cup  **cups**

hose  **hoses**

NEW SOUND - "ch"

Phonic Rules:
"t" is silent before "ch" (witch).
When two consonants with the same sound come together only one is sounded (che<u>rr</u>y).

"ch"
bench, chick, chair, cherry.

"tch"
itch, latch, match, pitch, witch.

chick

bench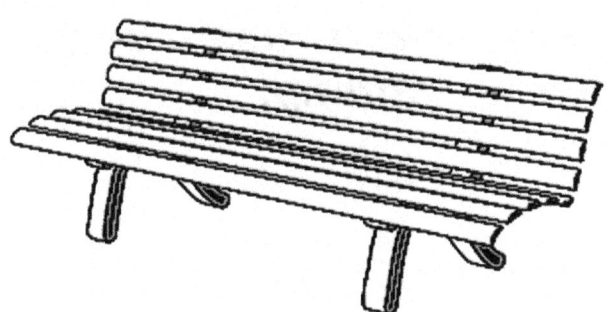

match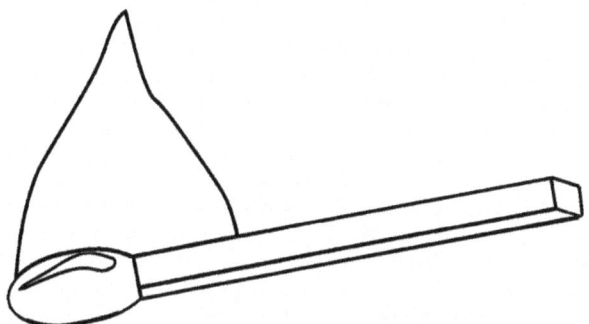

witch

NEW SOUND - "sh"

Phonic Rules:
Two consonants together "s" and "h" can form one sound that isn't like the sounds the letters are made from "sh".

"sh"
shoe, shell, ship, shall, shame, shed, shelf, ash, shop, shut, shave, cash, dash, mash, dish, wish, fish, rush, shrub, shrimp.

NEW SOUND - "th"

Phonic Rules:
There are two sounds for "th", voiced and voiceless "th".

"th" (voiceless) does not use vocal cords to say the word; sound passes between the tongue and teeth; "th" is at the beginning, middle or end of words that describe something: bath, thimble, thread, athlete, bathtub, teeth, moth.

"th" (voiced) uses vocal cords; "th" is between two vowels; functional sentence words that have no specific meaning or action; if "th" is followed by a silent "e" or between two vowels: bathe, the, that, then, there, their, this, these, them, thus, feather, lathe, mother, with, weather.

       bath (unvoiced) …… bathe (voiced)

Have children sound out the voiceless and voiced "th" sound above, so they can see the two different sounds of "th".

(voiced) ba_the_

(voiceless) ba_th_

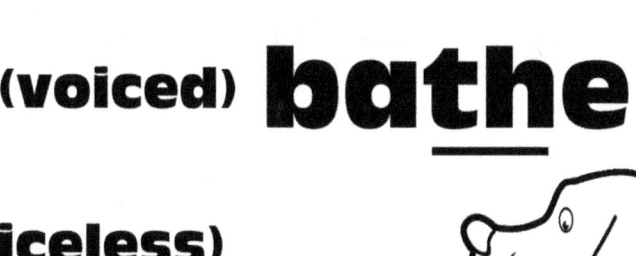

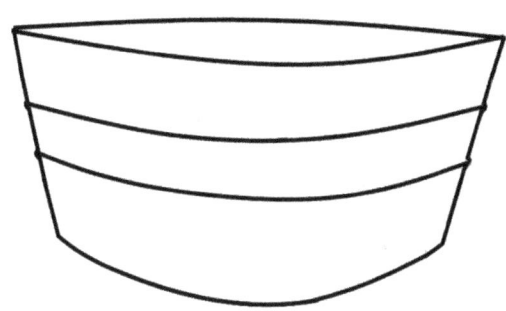

(voiced) fea_ther_

(voiceless) _th_imble

NEW SOUND - "wh"

Phonic Rules:
Two consonants "w" and "h" form one sound "wh".

"wh"
wheel, wheat, whale, when, which, while, white, whim, whistle.

whale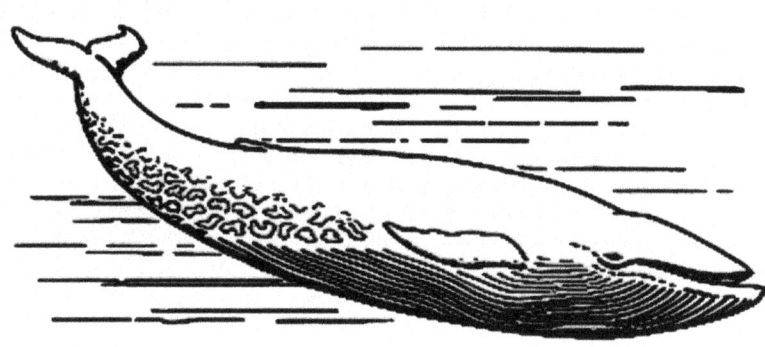

 **wheel**

wheat

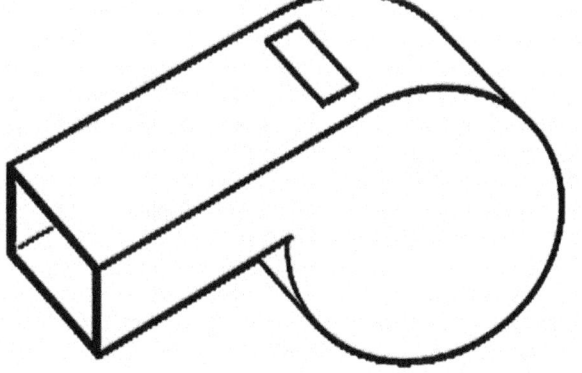 **whistle**

NEW SOUND - THREE SOUNDS OF "y"

Phonic Rules:
Three sounds of "y": yam, candy, my.
At the end of a word "y" makes the sound of long "e" or long "i".

"y"= short "y"
yam, yes, yet, yell, yelp, yolk, yoke.

"y"= long "e"
candy, cherry, windy, kitty, penny, chilly, sorry, sunny, puppy, empty, twenty, copy, foggy, bunny.

"y"= long "i"
by, my, cry, dry, fly, pry, spy, try, why, shy, sky, style.

yolk

yam

candy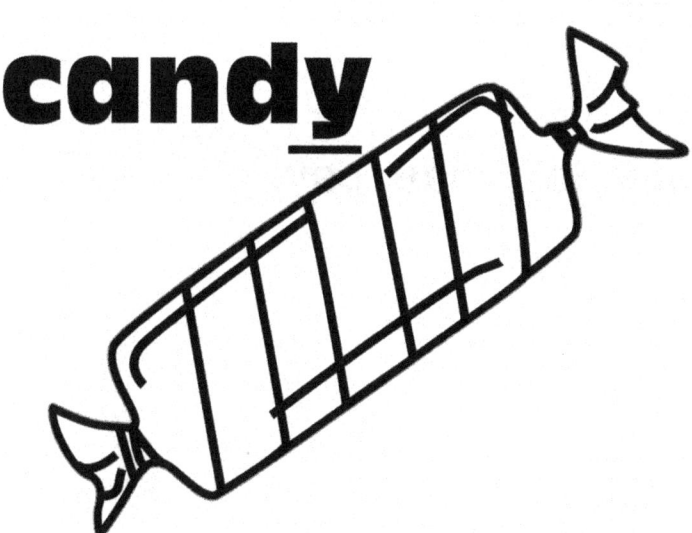

cherry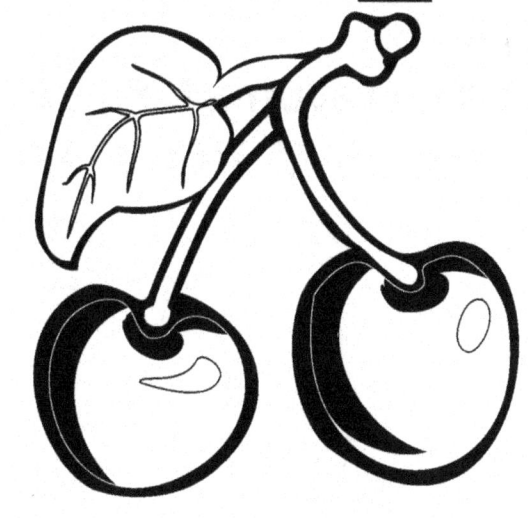

fly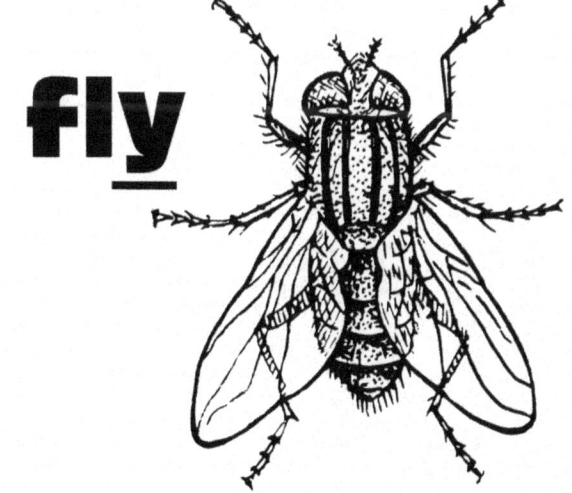

fry

NEW SOUND - "ai" and "ay"= long "a"

Phonic Rules:
When two vowels come together, the first vowel is usually long (says its name) and the second is silent.
"ai" two letter "A" that we do not use at the end of English words.
"ay" two letter "A" that we do use at the end of English words.

"ai"
aid, laid, maid, paid, rail, hail, jail, mail, nail, sail, snail, trail, claim, rain, drain, brain, train, chain, waist, wait.

"ay"
bay, crayons, hay, day, clay, lay, may, pay, play, say, stay, stray, way, pray.

ch<u>ai</u>n

 **tr<u>ai</u>n**

h<u>ay</u>

cr<u>ay</u>on

NEW SOUND - "ea" and "ee" = long "e"

Phonic Rules:
"ee" always says long "e"; "e" before a vowel makes the vowel say its name.

"ea"
sea, tea, flea, each, beach, peach, reach, teach, bead, lead, read, leaf, leak, beak, peak, speak, weak, heal, meal, seal, steal, beam, team, bean, stream.

"ee"
see, fee, bee, flee, free, three, tree, leech, speech, deed, feed, need, seed, weed, bleed, beef, seek, cheek, creek, eel, feel, heel, peel, steel, seem, seen, queen, sheep, sweep, deer.

p<u>ea</u>ch

<u>ea</u>r

b<u>ee</u>

sh<u>ee</u>p

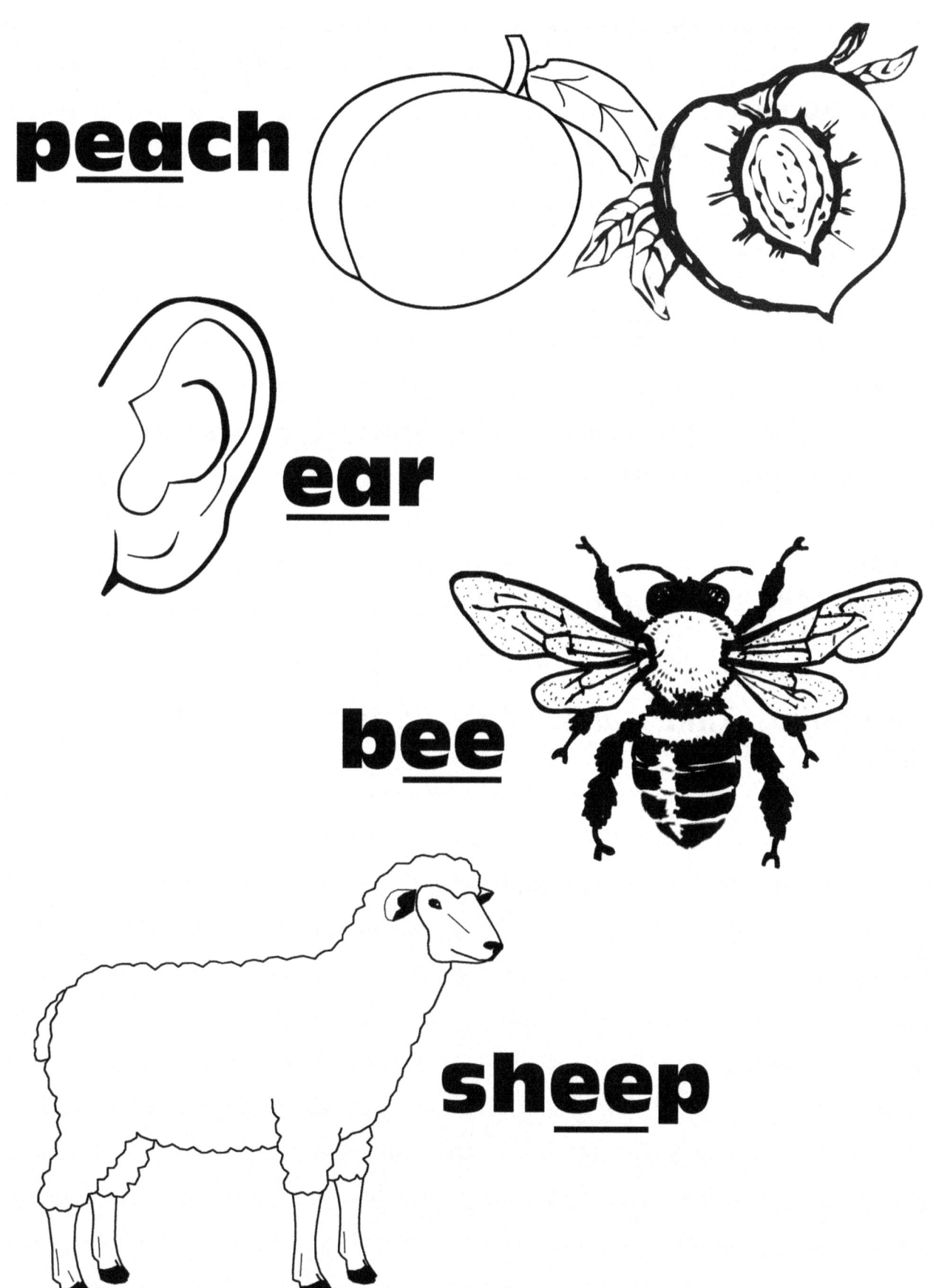

NEW SOUND - "ie" and "igh" = long "i"

Phonic Rules:
"i" is long when followed by "ld", "nd" or "gh".

"ie"
die, lie, pie, tie, diet, lied, pies, tied, fries, tries, diets, fiery, spies, skies.

"igh"
high, nigh, sigh, light, night, fight, right, sight, thigh, tight, fright, tights.

"ild"
mild, wild, child, mildly, wilder.

"ind"
bind, find, kind, mind, blinds, grind, winds, finder, kinder.

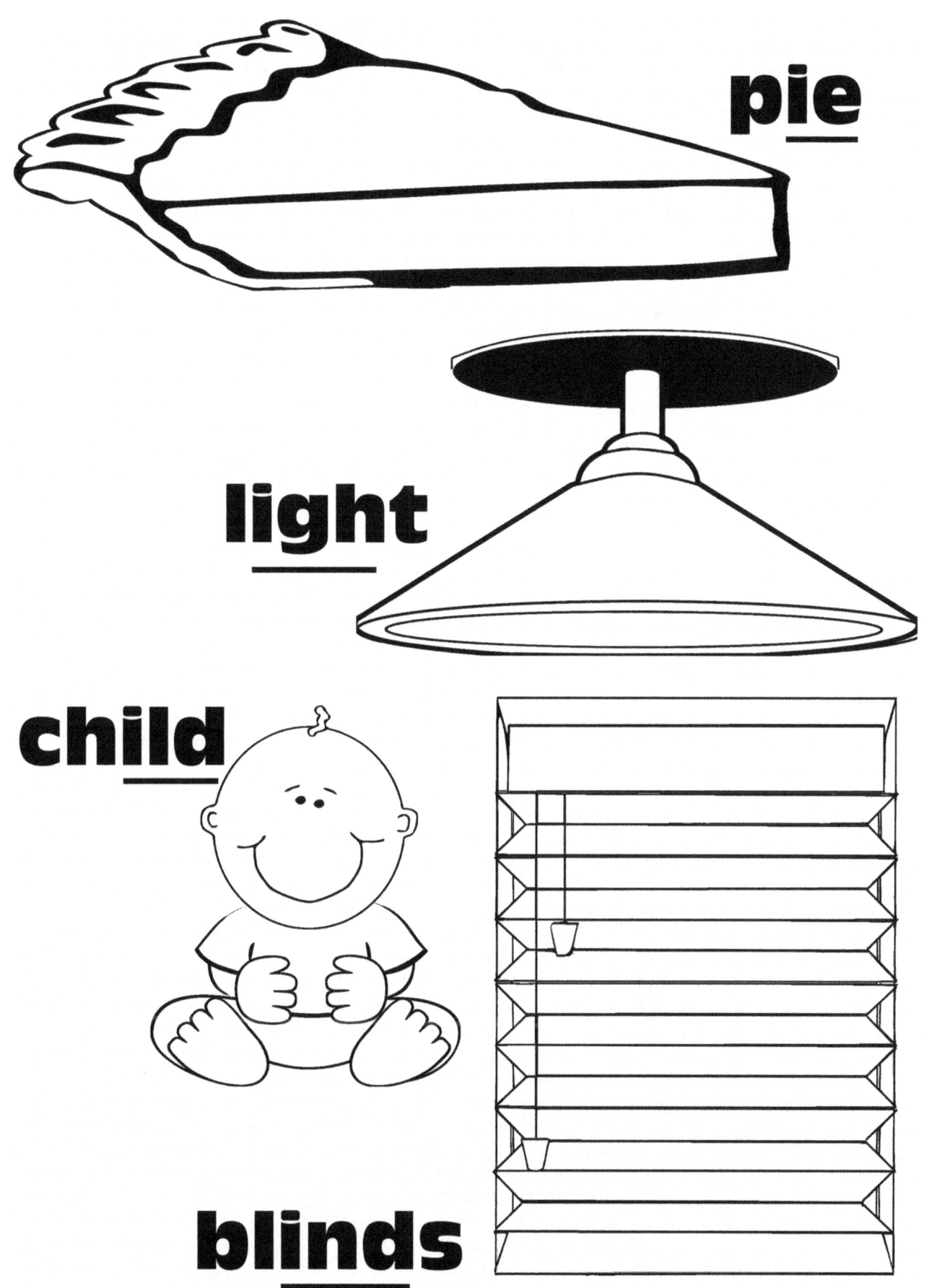

p<u>ie</u>

l<u>igh</u>t

ch<u>i</u>ld

bl<u>in</u>ds

NEW SOUND - "oa" and "oe" = long "o"

Phonic Rules:
"o" is long when followed by "ld".

"oa"
load, road, toad, loaf, coach, poach, roach, oak, cloak, croak, soak, coal, foam, roam, loan, goat, boat, throat, oar, soar, board, roast, toast.

"oe"
doe, hoe, joe, roe, toe, woe, does, goes, poem, poet, shoe, canoe.

"old"
told, cold, gold, hold, mold, sold, scold.

l<u>oa</u>f

g<u>oa</u>t

sh<u>oe</u>

g<u>o</u>ld

can<u>oe</u>

NEW SOUND - "ow" and "ou"= "ow"

Phonic Rules: You generally use the "ou" ("ow" sound) at the beginning and middle of a word; and the "ow" sound at the end of a word: ouch, couch, cow.

"ou"
couch, pouch, slouch, loud, cloud, proud, bound, found, mound, pound, round, ground, sound, count, mount, our, sour, scour, flour, house.

"ow"
owl, howl, fowl, growl, bow, brow, cow, how, now, plow, down, town, gown, clown, frown, crown, brown, drown, crowd, drowsy.

NEW SOUND-("ar" "ear" "ir" "or" "ur") = "er"

Phonic Rules:
"ar" "ear" "ir" "or" "ur" sounds that have the same "er" sound.

"ar"
ear, dear, earn, fear, gear, rear, liar.

"ear"
bear, earth, pearl, earn, learn.

"ir"
skirt, bird, girl, shirt.

"or"
doctor, sailor, word, world.

"ur"
nurse, purse, fur, turtle.

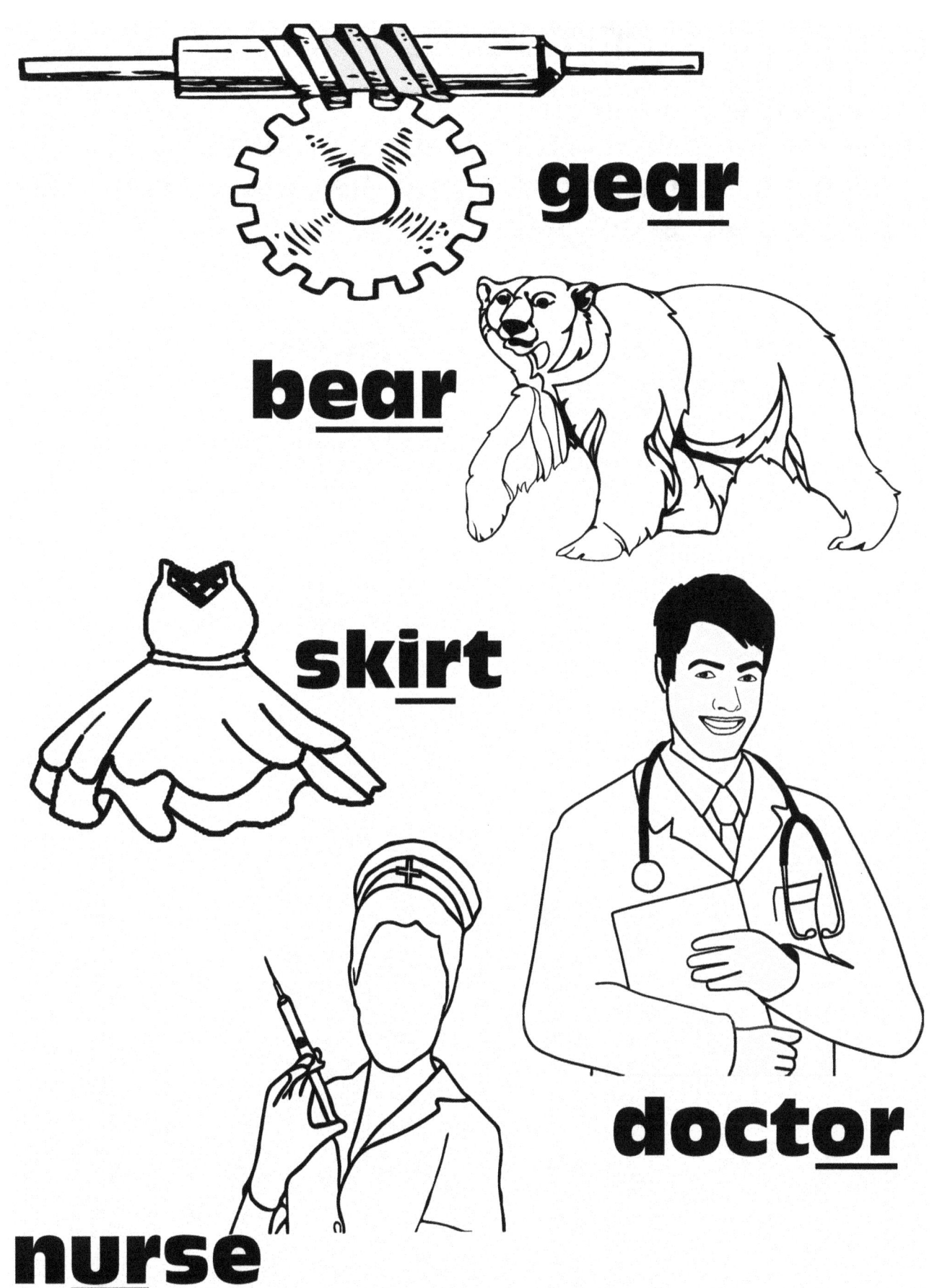

ge**ar**

b**ear**

sk**ir**t

doct**or**

n**ur**se

NEW SOUND - "kn" = "n"

Phonic Rules:
In some English words two written letters of a word have a single sound, with one of the letter sounds being silent; "k" is usually silent before "n".

"kn" = "n"
knob, knot, knee, knit, knife, know, known, knight, knock, knocking.

knit

knob

NEW SOUND - "gn" = "n"

Phonic Rules:
In some English words two written letters have a single sound, with one of the letter sounds being silent.
"g" is silent before "n".

"gn" = "n"
align, design, gnome, gnat, gnats, gnash, gnashes, gnaw, reign, sign.

gnat

gnome

NEW SOUND - "gu" = "g"

Phonic Rules:
In some English words two written letters of a word have a single sound, with one of the letter sounds being silent; the "u" in "gu" is usually silent.

"gu" = "g"
guess, guesses, guy, guide, guides, guided, guiding, guild, guilt, guilty, guest, guitar, plague, rogue, guard, tongue, morgue.

guitar

tongue

NEW SOUND - "wr" = "r"

Phonic Rules:
In some English words two written letters have a single sound, with one of the letter sounds being silent; the "w" in "wr" is usually silent.

"wr" = "r"
wrap, wren, wrench, wrenches, wring, wringer, wrist, wrong, write, writing, wrote, wreath, wreck, wrecks.

<u>w</u>renches

<u>w</u>reath

121

NEW SOUND - "mb" = "m"

Phonic Rules:
In some English words two written letters have a single sound, with one of the letter sounds being silent; if a word ends in "mb" the "b" is silent.

"mb" = "m"
lamb, limb, comb, climb, dumb, crumb, numb, plumbing, thumb.

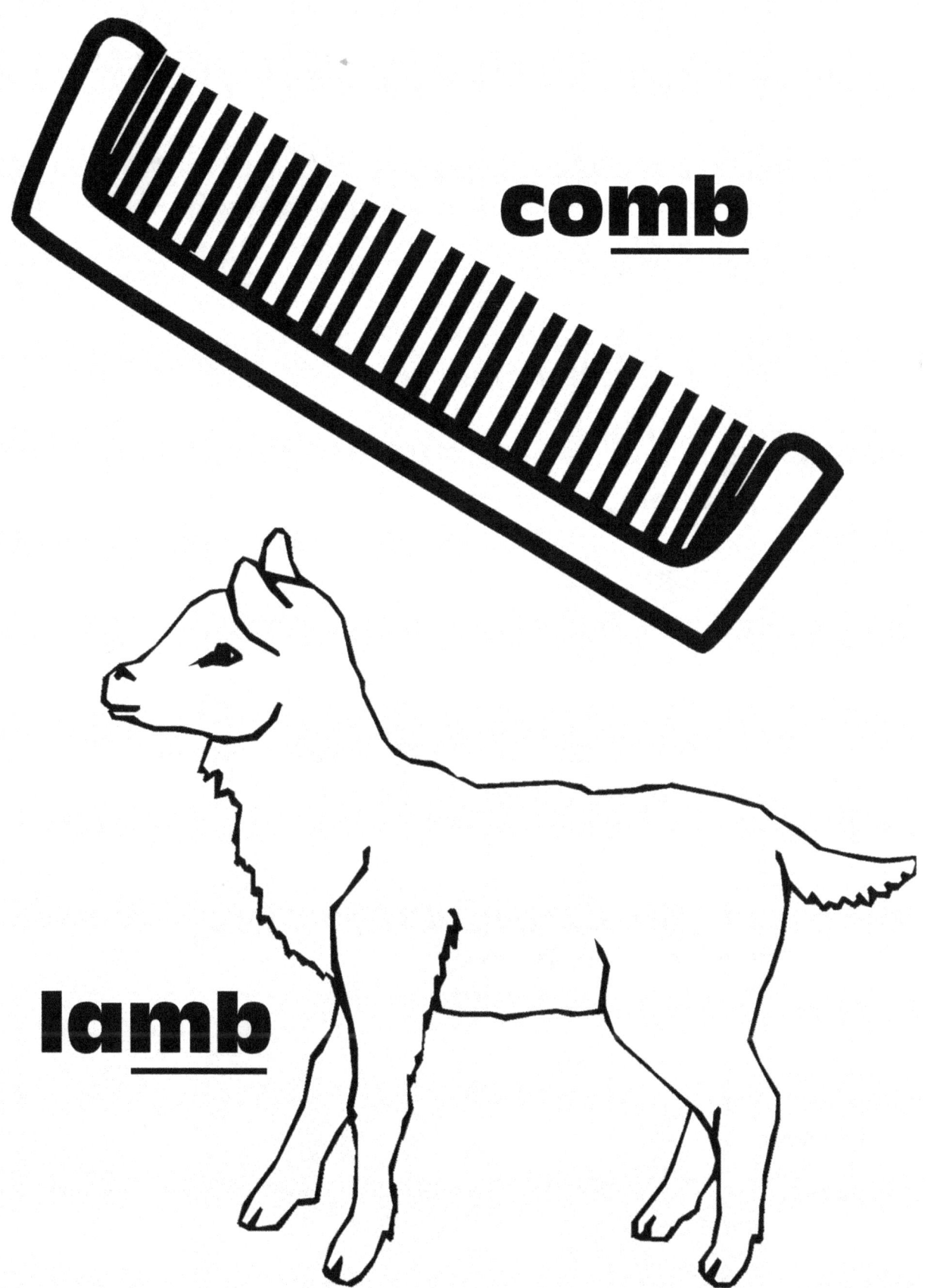

co**mb**

la**mb**

NEW SOUND "ai"= short "i" – "ea"= long "a" "ea"= short "e" – "ie"= long "e"

Phonic Rules:
"ai" not used at the end of a word, as English words do not end in "i" - "a" is silent and "i" says its short sound.
"ea" where "e" is silent and "a" says its name (long "A").
"ea" where "a" is silent and "e" says its short sound.
"ie" where "i" is silent and "e" says its name.

"ai"= short "i"
captain, fountain, mountain.

"ea"= long "a"
break, breakers, breaking, great, steak.

"ea"= short "e"
head, dead, read, ready, dread, bread, spread, thread, deaf, health, wealth, meant, feather.

"ie"= long "e"
chief, thief, thieves, brief, field, priest, tier, wield, yield, shield, grief, grieve, grieves.

NEW SOUND – "g" = "j" - "dge"

Phonic Rules:
"g" has the sound of "j" before "e", "i" or "y".
"dge" has the sound of "j".

"g" = "j" before "e" - "i" or "y"
gem, age, gage, page, hinge, fringe, angel.
aging, gig, gin, gist, engine, ginger, magic.
gym, edgy, dodgy, gymnast, gypsy.

"dge" = "j".
badge, edge, ledge, hedge, wedge, sledge, pledge, dredge, ridge, bridge, dodge, lodge, budge, nudge, judge.

NEW SOUND "oo"-"oe"-"ue"-"ou""ew"= "oo"

Phonic Rules:
"oo" "oe" "ue" "ou" "ew" all have the same sound as long "oo" as in boot.

"oo"
boot, hoof, roof, proof, cool, pool, tool, food, boom, gloom, moon, spoon, goose, broom.

"oe"
shoe, shoemaker, shoes.

"ue"
blue, cue, clue, flue, glue, true, value.

"ou"
soup, croup, group, grouped, wound.

"ew"
drew, grew, crew, screw, threw, chew.

NEW SOUND "oi" - "oy"

Phonic Rules:
"oi" and "oy" have the same sound; like "oy" in boy.

"oi"
oil, toil, soil, boil, spoil, coin, join, joint, point, moist, noise, noisy.

"oy"
boy, toy, joy, enjoy, joyful, oyster, boyhood.

oil

coin

toy

oyster

NEW SOUND "aw"-"au"-"augh"-"ough"= "aw"

Phonic Rules:
"aw"-"au"-"augh"-"ough" all make the sound of "aw" as in saw.

"aw"
saw, jaw, gnaw, law, claw, paw, hawk, draw, straw, thaw, awning, dawn, lawn, yawn.

"au"
auger, saucer, cause, gauze, pause, author.

"augh"
caught, taught, daughter, naughty, slaughter.

"ough"
ought, brought, fought, sought, thought, wrought, nought.

NEW SOUND "sh"

Phonic Rules:
"ce"-"ci"-"si"-"ti"-"sh" all have the same sound of "sh".

"ce"
ocean.

"ci"
musician, physician, precious, delicious, special.

"si"
excursion, permission, Russia.

"ti"
action, collection, correction, objection, station, nation, combination, relation, motion.

"sh"
ship, shell, shop, shave, ash, cash, dish, fish.

NEW SOUND "ph" and "gh" = "f"

Phonic Rules:
"ph" and "gh" have the same sound as "f" (as in phonics or laugh).

"ph"
telephone, telegraph, pheasant, photograph, phonics, orphan, sulphur, nephew, elephant, alphabet, geography.

"gh"
cough, coughing, trough, rough, roughest, tough, toughen, enough, laugh, laughing, laughter.

NEW SOUND "ei" - "ey" - "ew" - "eu" - "eigh"

Phonic Rules:
"ei" has three sounds, long "e" "a" and "i".
"ey" long "e" sound.
"ew" long "u" "oo" sound.
"eigh" long "a" sound

"ei"
being, beige, heist, reindeer, veil, vein, reins, reign.

"ey"
key, donkey, chimney, alley, valley, pulley.

"ew"
brew, chew, stew, steward, new, dew, few, flew, screw, renew, sew, news, newt, pew, grew, view, crew.

"eu"
feud, reuse, queue, neuter, neuron, museum, makeup, feudal, neutral, coliseum.

"eigh"
eight, weigh, weight, weighs, sleigh.

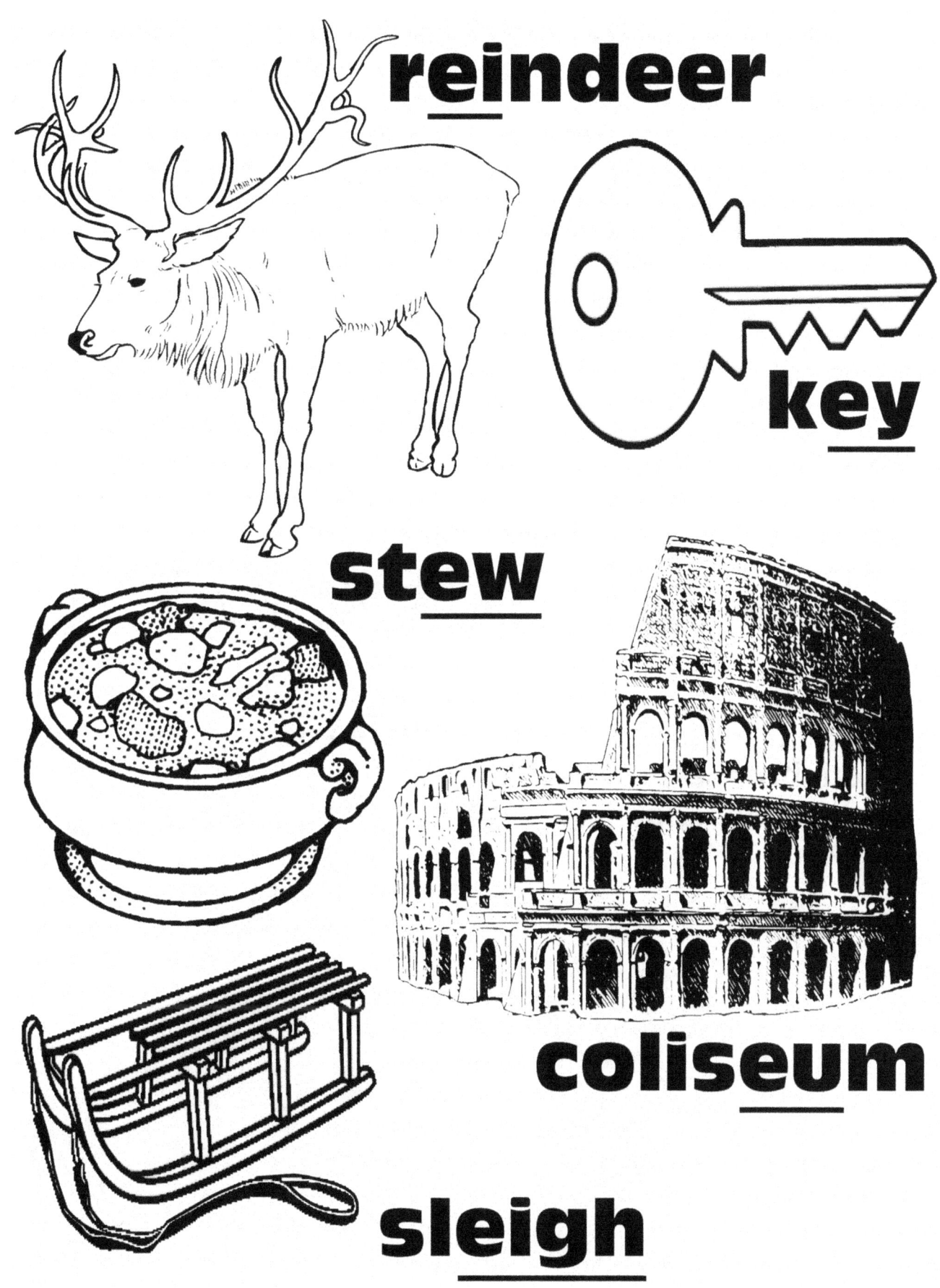

NEW SOUND-"ed"="ed"-"ed"="d"-"ed"="t"

Phonic Rules:
The "ed" sound is used when a word ends in "t" or "d" and shows something has happened in the past.
"ed" = "d" (voiced) word uses vocal cords.
"ed" = "t" (voiceless) word does not use vocal cords.

"ed" = "ed"
acted, adopted, blasted, heated, lifted, looted, melted, painted, planted, printed, salted, sanded, started, wanted.

"ed" = "d" (voiced) uses vocal cords.
aimed, buttered, canned, cleaned, climbed, drilled, filled, grilled, kneeled, loaned, played, plowed, pinned, sailed, sealed.

"ed" = "t" (voiceless) does not use vocal cords.
baked, brushed, choked, clapped, dressed, knocked, liked, packed, patched, puffed, reached, stamped, wrecked.

NEW SOUND - "ang"-"ong"-"ung"-"eng"

Phonic Rules:
"ang" all short letter sounds (bang); or long "a" and "j" sound (angel).
"eng" "g" says "j" (engine); or "g" is silent (length); or "g" is short and "j" (engage, engulf).

"ang"
hanger, bang, hang, gang, rang, angry, angle, slang.

"ang"
 angel.

"ong"
tongs, song, gong, strong, long, among, along, wrong.

"ung"
rung, stung, swung, hung, lung, sung, young, swung.

"eng"
engine, length, strength, engage, english, engulf.

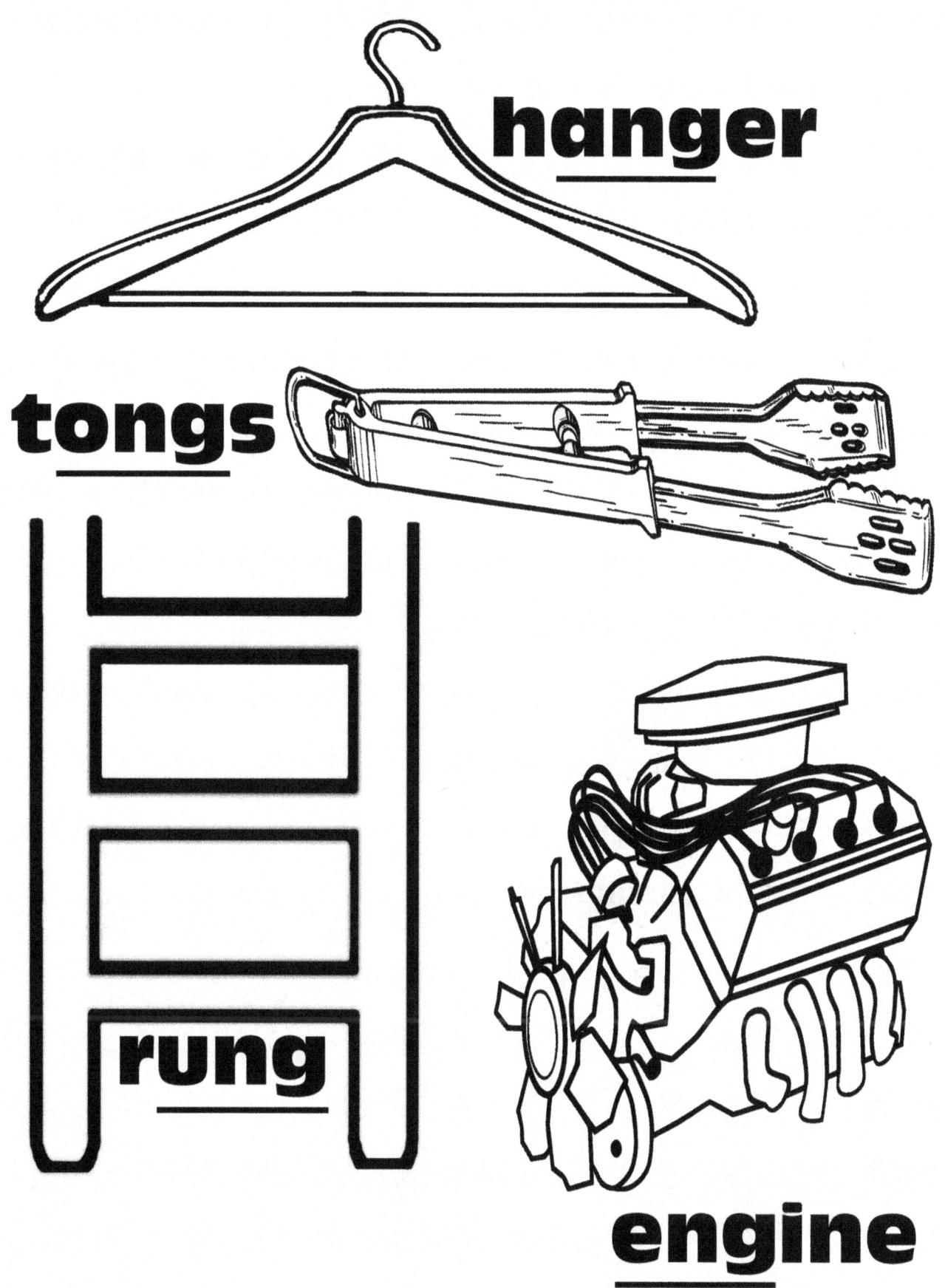

THIS BOOK TEACHES 76 SOUNDS

21 Consonants with their different sounds:
"b" (bed), "c" (cat, cell), "d" (dog), "f" (fan), "g" (gas, gem), "h" (hat), "j" (jam), "k" (keg), "l" (lab), "m" (mat), "n" (nun), "p" (pin), "q" (queen, que), "r" (rat), "s" (sun, easy), "t" (tap), "v" (van), "w" (web), "x" (fox, xray), "y" (yak, buy, any, hymn), "z" (zoo).

5 Vowels:
"a" (apple, cake, yacht, ball, chair), "e" (elephant, eagle), "i" (insect, pie, patio), "o" (octopus, overcoat, owl, oven), "u" (umbrella, unicorn, urn).

Short and Long Vowels:

"a" -	can	cane
"e" -	met	meter
"i" -	pin	pine
"o" -	rob	robe
"u" -	cub	cube

50 Blended Consonants:
"ch", "sh", "th", "wh", "ai", "ay", "ea", "ee", "ie", "oe", "oa", "ue", "igh", "ow", "ou", "er", "ang", "ong", "ung", "eng", "kn", "wr", "mb", "gu", "gn", "dge", "oo", "oy", "oi", "or", "ar", "ear", "ir", "er", "aw", "au", "ed", "ph", "ti", "si", "ci", "ei", "ey", "ew", "ough", "augh", "gh", "eu", "eigh", "ce".

Note: extra words are shown where a letter has more than one sound.

TEACHING TIPS

The goal of phonics is to show beginning readers how to decode written words by learning the lowercase or short letter sounds and making those sounds into words.

You are teaching:
1. The 21 lowercase (short) sounds of a letter first.
2. 5 vowels that have a short and long sounds.
3. 50 most common blended consonant sounds (digraphs).
4. Sight words.
5. Phonic rules.

Sight Words, or Whole Language is usually words with alphabet letter sounds that cannot be sounded out phonetically.

Do not rush your child; take your time and only teach one or two concepts at a time; for preschoolers under 3 only spend 10 minutes on each letter sound; learning should be fun; see the book "Play Based Ways To Teach Your Child To Read", which shows you what play based materials to use to teach your child to read.

Where possible, all picture words in this book can be sounded out using the lower case or short sound of an alphabet letter.

Picture words and blended consonants (digraphs) that cannot be sounded out using the short sound of an alphabet letter are underlined; you teach these words as sight words.

Where possible three letter words in this book have two consonants and one short sounding vowel.

Single phonemes (the Alphabet letter sounds "a" to "z") may have more than one sound; let your child know that some letters have more than one sound.

When your child masters the single short letter sounds of the alphabet you can introduce all the vowel sounds and digraphs, which are two or more letters spelling and making one sound, such as "ch" or "sh"; the digraph is the letters and phonemes are the sound; teach digraphs as sight words; and only one at a time, until your child has mastered the blended sound.

As your child becomes more familiar with reading 3 letter words and digraphs you can introduce the phonic rules.

Pages of this book (where possible) list phonetic sounding words; phonic rules and sight words are at the back of this book.

When teaching your child to read, start with:
1. Ear Training.
2. Tongue Training
3. Eye Training.
4. 21 consonant short Alphabet letter sounds.
5. 5 vowel sounds.
6. Diagraphs (two or more letters with one sound).
7. The Names (capital) Letters of The Alphabet.
8. Phonic Rules.

People's dialects and accents may affect how an English alphabet letter and word sounds?

It is recommended that you do not teach the name (capital, long, or uppercase) sound of a letter until your child has mastered the lowercase (short) alphabet letter sounds.

Most three letter words will have a Consonant - Vowel - Consonant (CVC), so practice with your child blending the consonant alphabet letters with the 5 vowels and other consonants: "b"at"; "b"et; "b"it; "b"og "b"ut; or "d"ab; "d"en; "d"ip; "d"ot; "d"ug.

Short sentence readers are best in a step by step progressive order:

- Two words which have three or four letters that can be sounded out phonetically (their lowercase letter sound); no punctuation or capitals.
- Three words which have three or four letters that can be sounded out phonetically: no punctuation or capitals.
- Four words which have three, four or more letters that can be sounded out phonetically with punctuation, capitals and sight words.
- Introduction of pre and primer (up to 5 years) sight words that cannot be sounded out phonetically.
- Complete sentences with sight words, capitals and punctuation.
- Black and white, line drawn pictures.

SHORT SENTENCE READERS

If your child has mastered Fast Start For Early Readers - Kindergarten, they are ready for Fast Start For Early Readers Level 1

FAST START FOR EARLY READERS LEVEL 1: Children learn to read two-and three-word sentences that can be sounded out with their lowercase phonetic sound; and recognize some of the Pre-Primer Sight Words.

Early Readers: should start with a single word; then two words or more; all words should be lowercase short letters and where possible be able to be sounded out phonetically; pictures should be black and white, or a color picture without a background.

FAST START FOR EARLY READERS LEVEL 2: teaches children to read (where possible) with phonetically sounding letter words and punctuated sentences.

Your child will learn 92 pre-primer Sight Words and how to make short sentences.

Pre-primer: (40 words) a, and, away, big, blue, can, come, down, find, for, funny, go, help, here, I, in, is, it, jump, little, look, make, me, my, not, one, play, red, run, said, see, the, three, to, two, up, we, where, yellow, you.

Primer: (52 words) all, am, are, at, ate, be, black, brown, but, came, did, do, eat, four, get, good, have, he, into, like, must, new, no, now, on, our, out, please, pretty, ran, ride, saw, say, she, so, soon, that, there, they, this, too, under, want, was, well, went, what, white, who, will, with, yes.

Let your child know that Sight Words, or words that cannot be sounded out using letter sounds are underlined; some sight words can be sounded out.

PHONIC RULES and SIGHT WORDS:

LETTER "a"
PHONIC RULES:
Letter "a" can have five sounds, **a**pple, c**a**ke, y**a**ught, b**a**ll, ch**a**ir.
"ai" 2 letter "A" that we do not use at the end of English words (afraid).
"ay" 2 letter "A" that we do use at the end of English words (away).
"ai" and "ay"= long "a" (afraid, away).
"a", "aw", "au", "augh"="aw" (all, saw, pause, caught).

Sight Words: a, and, away, all, am, are, at, ate.

LETTER "b"
PHONIC RULES:
When "*e*" is the last letter in a word, the first vowel usually says its name and the *e* is silent; as in blue.
"bu"="b" (**bu**ild, **bu**ys).
"bt"="t" (dou**bt**, de**bt**).

Sight Words: big, blue, be, black, brown, but.

LETTER "c"
PHONIC RULES:
"c" says "s" if before "e", "i" or "y" (**c**ity, **c**ent, **c**yst).
"ce" and "ci"= "sh" (ocean, special).

Sight Words: can, come, came.

LETTER "d"
PHONIC RULES:
"ir" the er of "d<u>ir</u>t".
"dg"="j" (ba<u>dg</u>e, do<u>dg</u>e).

Sight Words: down, did, do.

LETTER "e"
PHONIC RULES:
When 2 vowels are together the first often says its name and the second is silent (<u>ea</u>t).
Double "ee" always says "E" (b<u>ee</u>).
"ea" and "ee"= long "e" (t<u>ea</u>, s<u>ee</u>).
Final "e" is dropped when "ing" is added (driv<u>e</u> becomes driving).

Sight Words: eat.

LETTER "f"
PHONIC RULES:
If a vowel is followed by an "*r*" (four) the vowel may make a new sound "or",
"ph" and "gh"="f" (<u>ph</u>onics, tou<u>gh</u>).

Sight Words: find, for, funny, four.

LETTER "g"
PHONIC RULES:
"g" before "e", "i", or "y" may say "j" (<u>g</u>ent's).
"gu"="g" (<u>gu</u>ess, <u>gu</u>ide).
"gn"="n" (<u>gn</u>at, si<u>gn</u>).

Sight Words: go, get, good.

LETTER "h"
PHONIC RULES:
"er" the er of "her"
Final "e" is silent and usually makes the preceding vowel say its name (h<u>e</u>re, h<u>o</u>me); "have" is an exception.

Sight Words: help, here, have, he.

LETTER "i"
PHONIC RULES:
"i" before "e" except after "c".
"ie" and "igh"= long "i" (t<u>ie</u>. s<u>igh</u>t).

Sight Words: I, in, is, it, into.

LETTER "j"
PHONIC RULES:
Two consonants together (th) can form one sound that isn't like the sounds the letters are made from (<u>th</u>e).
Two consonants can have the same sound "c"="k" (ja<u>ck</u>et).

Sight Words: jump.

LETTER "k"
PHONIC RULES:
When "r" comes after a vowel the vowel is silent and says "r" as in kart.
"kn"="n" (<u>kn</u>ife, <u>kn</u>ee).
"ch" and "qu"="k" (a<u>ch</u>e, s<u>ch</u>ool; mos<u>qu</u>ito, con<u>qu</u>er).

Sight Words: 0

LETTER "l"
PHONIC RULES:
"mb"="m" (la<u>mb</u>, cli<u>mb</u>).
Two of the same consonants together have the same single sound (la<u>dd</u>er).
"tle"="l" (lit<u>tle</u>).

Sight Words: look, little, like.

LETTER "m"
PHONIC RULES:
"y"= long "i" (m<u>y</u>).
Final "e" is silent and often makes the preceding vowel say its name (m<u>a</u>ke).

Sight Words: make, me, my, must.

LETTER "n"
PHONIC RULES:
"ew"= long "u" (new).
"en", "in", "on", "ten" = "n" (op<u>en</u>, bas<u>in</u>, butt<u>on</u>, of<u>ten</u>).

Sight Words: not, new, no, now.

LETTER "o"
PHONIC RULES:
"oa" and "oe"= long "o" (r<u>oa</u>d, t<u>oe</u>).
"ow" and "ou"= ow (<u>ow</u>l, l<u>ou</u>d).
"ow" and "ou"= long "o" (b<u>ow</u>, s<u>ou</u>l).

Sight Words: one, on, our, out.

LETTER "p"
PHONIC RULES:
Say two consonants as one sound "pl" (<u>pl</u>ease, <u>pl</u>ay); "pr" (<u>pr</u>etty).
"ea"= long "e" (pl<u>ea</u>se).
"ay"= long "a" (pl<u>ay</u>).

Sight Words: play, please, pretty.

LETTER "q"
PHONIC RULES:
"q" is usually written as "qu" but is pronounced "kw".
"qu"="k" (mos<u>qu</u>ito, con<u>qu</u>er).

Sight Words: 0

LETTER "r"
PHONIC RULES:
"ar", "ear", "ir", "or", and "ur" all say "er" (doll<u>ar</u>, <u>ear</u>th, b<u>ir</u>d, w<u>or</u>k, f<u>ur</u>).
A vowel is long when one consonant is between it and the next vowel (r<u>ide</u>).

Sight Words: red, run, ran, ride.

LETTER "s"
PHONIC RULES:
"s" often has the sound of "z" (shine<u>s</u>).
Two consonants form one sound "sh" (<u>sh</u>e, <u>sh</u>ines).
"si"="sh" (permis<u>si</u>on).

Sight Words: said, see, saw, say, she, so, soon.

LETTER "t"
PHONIC RULES:
Voiced and voiceless sound of "th"; voiced words that have no specific meaning (<u>th</u>at, <u>th</u>ere, <u>th</u>ey); voiceless content, noun, verb words (<u>th</u>ree).

Sight Words: the, three, to, two, that, there, they, this, too.

LETTER "u"
PHONIC RULES:
When two consonants having the same sound come together, only one is sounded (umbre<u>ll</u>a, bla<u>ck</u>).
"o", "ou" and "oo"= short "u" (s<u>o</u>n, y<u>ou</u>ng, fl<u>oo</u>d).
"ue"= long "u" (c<u>ue</u>, d<u>ue</u>).
A vowel is short when there are two consonants with the same sound between it and the next vowel (umbre<u>ll</u>a).

Sight Words: up, under.

LETTER "v"
PHONIC RULES:
Apostrophe "'s" shows ownership (vet's).

Sight Words: 0

LETTER "w"
PHONIC RULES:
"wr"="r" (<u>wr</u>ap, <u>wr</u>ench).
"t" is silent before "ch" (wi<u>tch</u>).

Sight Words: we, where, want, was, well, went, what, white, who, will, with.

LETTER "x"
PHONIC RULES:
"x"="ks".
A vowel is short when there are two or more different consonants between it and the next vowel (ex**t**r**a**).
Two consonants form one sound "sh" (**sh**ows).
"ex" = "egz" (**ex**am).

Sight Words: 0

LETTER "y".
PHONIC RULES:
"y" has 3 sounds: "y" as in **y**ellow; "E" as in pupp**y**; and "I" as in tr**y**.
"y" sounds like "e" (ver**y**).

Sight Words: yellow, you, yes

LETTER "z"
PHONIC RULES:
A vowel is long when there is one consonant between it and the next vowel (z**e**ro, p**a**per).
"s" often has the sound of "z" (wa**s**).

Sight Words: 0

OTHER BOOKS BY THE AUTHOR

Buy these books at: http://howtoteachchildrentoread.ca

HOW TO TEACH CHILDREN TO READ
This book introduces children to 86 phonetic sounds of the English language in a step by step plan to teach a child of any age to read. How To Teach Children To Read also introduces the 220 Dolch word list (sight words) so that a child will be able to read, write and spell most written words.

TEACH YOUR CHILD TO READ – ALPHABET AND THREE LETTER WORDS
This book introduces 26 alphabet letter sounds and shows children how to read and write three letter words.
A preschool child learns the 26 basic phonetic sounds of the English alphabet; how to read and write most three letter words; and that alphabet letter sounds form words written in books.

TEACH YOUR CHILD TO READ – VOWELS-PHONICS and SIGHT WORDS
This book is the second step in a preschool child learning to read.
Children will learn 60 blended phonetic sounds; 220 Dolch Sight Words; how to read and write three, four or more letter words using a play-based method to teach a preschool child how to read.

TEACH YOUR CHILD TO READ – ALPHABET PHONICS SHORT SENTENCES
Third Book in the "Teach Your Child To Read" series. Children learn how alphabet sounds form words; how to read three - and four-letter words; how to read short sentences; the most common Sight Words; blended consonant sounds and that reading can be fun.

OTHER BOOKS BY THE AUTHOR
Buy these books at: http://howtoteachchildrentoread.ca

	**PLAY-BASED WAYS TO TEACH YOUR CHILD TO READ** This book shows you what play based toys and learning to read materials to use; a step by step plan to teach your child to read and write; how to present learning to read materials to your child; how to set up the in home reading and writing environment; that preschool children can learn to read and write.
	**LEO LEARNS TO READ** A "Teach Your Child To Read Story." Join Leo the lion on a journey to the library with his jungle friends; on the way to the library, Leo hides a secret he does not want his friends to know. Children learn the fundamentals keys of reading, and that learning to read helps us read to learn. An ideal picture story to read to your children to help them learn about reading.
	**ALPHABET PARK – A STORY TEACHING CHILDREN HOW TO READ** This story book teaches children the alphabet; what alphabet letters sound like; that letter sounds form words and words describe things; that nouns are the names of things; how to use imagination; communication skills; about feelings and values; developmental movement activities; starting to write the letter sounds; starting to write pre-primer Sight Words.
	**A WALK IN THE JUNGLE** Prepare preschool children emotionally, intellectually and physically, before they go to grade school. Give your child an unprecedented, LIFELONG advantage, simply by reading them a storybook; a storybook UNLIKE ANY OTHER you've seen before. It feels so good to see your child achieve milestones, absorb knowledge like a sponge and develop a true love of learning.

OTHER BOOKS BY THE AUTHOR

Buy these books at: http://howtoteachchildrentoread.ca

HOW TO TEACH CHILDREN TO READ
This book introduces children to 86 phonetic sounds of the English language in a step by step plan to teach a child of any age to read. How To Teach Children To Read also introduces the 220 Dolch word list (sight words) so that a child will be able to read, write and spell most written words.

TEACH YOUR CHILD TO READ – ALPHABET AND THREE LETTER WORDS
This book introduces 26 alphabet letter sounds and shows children how to read and write three letter words.
A preschool child learns the 26 basic phonetic sounds of the English alphabet; how to read and write most three letter words; and that alphabet letter sounds form words written in books.

TEACH YOUR CHILD TO READ – VOWELS- PHONICS and SIGHT WORDS
This book is the second step in a preschool child learning to read.
Children will learn 60 blended phonetic sounds; 220 Dolch Sight Words; how to read and write three, four or more letter words using a play-based method to teach a preschool child how to read.

TEACH YOUR CHILD TO READ – ALPHABET PHONICS SHORT SENTENCES
Third Book in the "Teach Your Child To Read" series. Children learn how alphabet sounds form words; how to read three - and four-letter words; how to read short sentences; the most common Sight Words; blended consonant sounds and that reading can be fun.

OTHER BOOKS BY THE AUTHOR
Buy these books at: http://howtoteachchildrentoread.ca

PLAY-BASED WAYS TO TEACH YOUR CHILD TO READ
This book shows you what play based toys and learning to read materials to use; a step by step plan to teach your child to read and write; how to present learning to read materials to your child; how to set up the in home reading and writing environment; that preschool children can learn to read and write.

LEO LEARNS TO READ
A "Teach Your Child To Read Story." Join Leo the lion on a journey to the library with his jungle friends; on the way to the library, Leo hides a secret he does not want his friends to know. Children learn the fundamentals keys of reading, and that learning to read helps us read to learn. An ideal picture story to read to your children to help them learn about reading.

ALPHABET PARK – A STORY TEACHING CHILDREN HOW TO READ
This story book teaches children the alphabet; what alphabet letters sound like; that letter sounds form words and words describe things; that nouns are the names of things; how to use imagination; communication skills; about feelings and values; developmental movement activities; starting to write the letter sounds; starting to write pre-primer Sight Words.

A WALK IN THE JUNGLE
Prepare preschool children emotionally, intellectually and physically, before they go to grade school. Give your child an unprecedented, LIFELONG advantage, simply by reading them a storybook; a storybook UNLIKE ANY OTHER you've seen before. It feels so good to see your child achieve milestones, absorb knowledge like a sponge and develop a true love of learning.

OTHER BOOKS BY THE AUTHOR
Buy these books at: http://howtoteachchildrentoread.ca

	**GORDY VISITS THE MOUTAINS** Gordy Visits The Mountains: helps children develop physical coordination, improves self-direction, enhances decision making, promotes problem solving. A fun play-based child development storybook activity gets your child ready to learn.
	**ALPHABETIC PHONICS - FAST START FOR EARLY READERS LEVEL 1** Once a pre-school child has learned the 26-alphabet letter sounds, 60 phonogram blended consonant sounds and the Pre-primer Sight Words, it is time to introduce short sentence readers of two, three, four or more words. In Alphabetic Phonics - Fast Start For Early Readers Level 1 children sound out the alphabet letter sounds to form two and three letter words.
	**ALPHABETIC PHONICS - FAST START FOR EARLY READERS LEVEL 2** Children have learned to sound out and read two and three letter words in level 1, in level 2 they are introduced to four or more words; capitals; punctation of a sentence; and pre and primer Sight Words to create sentences.
	**EDUCATIONAL CHILD'S PLAY** Play-based Child Development Activities. Prepare pre-school children emotionally, intellectually and physically, before they start school. A book jammed packed with play-based child development activities.

OTHER BOOKS BY THE AUTHOR
Buy these books at: http://howtoteachchildrentoread.ca

	**PRE SCHOOL COLORING AND PUZZLE BOOK** This coloring book is designed to help pre-school children with the following possible benefits: increase creativity; a free time activity; a transitional activity; a soothing distraction; improve fine motor skills; calm and center the mind; stimulate the brain and the senses; help focus the mind in the moment; take the mind off distracting thoughts.
	**ADULT AND CHILDREN COLORING BOOK** A 128 page adult and children coloring and puzzle book. The pictures and puzzles are printable for any age group, from adult coloring to children. This book was designed for my 42-year-old daughter who had a stroke and has limited movement and communication due to her stroke. This book is helping her use both hands, better her fine motor skills, and improve logical thinking skills.
	**MOTIVATIONAL COLORING PUZZLE BOOK** This book has inspirational pictures, comic art, and puzzles for children, adults and seniors. It is the Author's hope readers may experience some of the following benefits: Give children a calming activity. Help children learn to read and write. Increase your creativity. Challenge your thinking skills. Reduce stress. Improve your state of wellness. Improve fine motor skills. Calm and center the mind in the moment.
	**WORKPLACE STRESS MANAGEMENT** Do you feel stressed and anxious at work? You're about to discover easy to do workplace stress management activities to reduce stress, anxiety, and the possibility of a nervous breakdown in the workplace. You will Learn: a 5-minute exercise to start and finish your day; practical, easy to learn movements to help reduce workplace stress and anxiety.

OTHER BOOKS BY THE AUTHOR
Buy these books at: http://howtoteachchildrentoread.ca

	**GETTING THROUGH YOUR DAY** Getting Through Your Day Motivational Activities to help you reduce stress, be alert, in the moment, energized, and living a full life. This book introduces you to a 5-minute movement-based exercise to start your day. You will learn to focus the mind, energize the body, and be ready for a meaningful day.
	**FUN DAY FOR SENIORS** Thousands of activities to help seniors be alert, in the moment, energized and living a full life.

ABOUT THE AUTHOR

The author (Paul Mackie) has over twenty years of experience working with children and adults as an educator, and personal care worker.

Paul is a certified Early Childhood Educator in British Columbia, and a level two Early Childhood Educator in Alberta Canada.

Paul has worked as a Community Care worker with special needs children, adults and seniors; and has worked with children in daycares, day programs, and the school system.

The author has had several careers, with certification as a Marine Engineer; Industrial Millwright, Welder; Early Childhood Educator; with experience as a Teacher's Assistant; special needs childcare worker; Brain Gym Instructor; Senior Building Manager; with courses of study such as "The Writing Road to Reading", "Accelerated Learning" and other brain development courses.

The author is now retired from his final working position as Senior Building Manager for a non-profit housing society.

Paul Mackie is now a retired full-time author; who presents seminars on how to teach pre-school children how to read; and how to help pre-school children be the best that they can be using developmental movements and sensory activities.

http://howtoteachchildrentoread.ca